DATE DUE

**1st EDITION**

# Perspectives on Diseases and Disorders

## Multiple Sclerosis

Clay Farris Naff
*Book Editor*

D                                                    ondon

GALE
CENGAGE Learning™

Christine Nasso, *Publisher*
Elizabeth Des Chenes, *Managing Editor*

© 2009 Greenhaven Press, a part of Gale, Cengage Learning

Gale and Greenhaven Press are registered trademarks used herein under license.

*For more information, contact:*
Greenhaven Press
27500 Drake Rd.
Farmington Hills, MI 48331-3535
Or you can visit our Internet site at gale.cengage.com

Articles in Greenhaven Press anthologies are often edited for length to meet page requirements. In addition, original titles of these works are changed to clearly present the main thesis and to explicitly indicate the author's opinion. Every effort is made to ensure that Greenhaven Press accurately reflects the original intent of the authors. Every effort has been made to trace the owners of copyrighted material.

Cover image Bryson Biomedical Illustrations/Custom Medical Stock Photo, Inc. Reproduced by permission.

LIBRARY OF CONGRESS CATALOGING-IN-PUBLICATION DATA

Multiple Sclerosis / Clay Farris Naff, book editor.
    p. cm. -- (Perspectives on diseases and disorders)
  Includes bibliographical references and index.
  ISBN 978-0-7377-4381-4 (hardcover)
 1. Multiple sclerosis--Juvenile literature.  I. Naff, Clay Farris.
  RC377.M8392 2009
  616.8'34--dc22

                                                        2009002456

Printed in the United States of America
  2  3  4  5  6  7  13  12  11  10  09

# CONTENTS

# FOREWORD

"Medicine, to produce health, has to examine disease."
—Plutarch

Independent research on a health issue is often the first step to complement discussions with a physician. But locating accurate, well-organized, understandable medical information can be a challenge. A simple Internet search on terms such as "cancer" or "diabetes," for example, returns an intimidating number of results. Sifting through the results can be daunting, particularly when some of the information is inconsistent or even contradictory. The Greenhaven Press series Perspectives on Diseases and Disorders offers a solution to the often overwhelming nature of researching diseases and disorders.

From the clinical to the personal, titles in the Perspectives on Diseases and Disorders series provide student and other researchers with authoritative, accessible information in unique anthologies that include basic information about the disease or disorder, controversial aspects of diagnosis and treatment, and first-person accounts of those impacted by the disease. The result is a well-rounded combination of primary and secondary sources that, together, provide the reader with a better understanding of the disease or disorder.

Each volume in Perspectives on Diseases and Disorders explores a particular disease or disorder in detail. Material for each volume is carefully selected from a wide range of sources, including encyclopedias, journals, newspapers, nonfiction books, speeches, government documents, pamphlets, organization newsletters, and position papers. Articles in the first chapter provide an authoritative, up-to-date overview that covers symptoms, causes and effects, treatments, cures, and medical advances. The second chapter presents a substantial number of opposing viewpoints on controversial treatments and other current debates relating to the volume topic. The third chapter offers a variety of personal perspectives on the disease or disorder. Patients, doctors, caregivers, and loved ones represent just some of the voices found in this narrative chapter.

Each Perspectives on Diseases and Disorders volume also includes:

- An annotated **table of contents** that provides a brief summary of each article in the volume.
- An **introduction** specific to the volume topic.
- Full-color **charts and graphs** to illustrate key points, concepts, and theories.
- Full-color **photos** that show aspects of the disease or disorder and enhance textual material.
- **"Fast Facts"** that highlight pertinent additional statistics and surprising points.
- A **glossary** providing users with definitions of important terms.
- A **chronology** of important dates relating to the disease or disorder.
- An annotated list of **organizations to contact** for students and other readers seeking additional information.
- A **bibliography** of additional books and periodicals for further research.
- A detailed **subject index** that allows readers to quickly find the information they need.

Whether a student researching a disorder, a patient recently diagnosed with a disease, or an individual who simply wants to learn more about a particular disease or disorder, a reader who turns to Perspectives on Diseases and Disorders will find a wealth of information in each volume that offers not only basic information, but also vigorous debate from multiple perspectives.

# INTRODUCTION

To most it feels like a death sentence. A diagnosis of multiple sclerosis (MS) opens a truly bleak prospect. Psychiatric nurse Joan Carter recalls her reaction: "I will never forget the day my neurologist gave me the possible diagnosis. . . . It was like the world was coming to an end."[1]

Multiple sclerosis develops as a person's immune system destroys the protective covering on nerve pathways. The disease gradually robs a person of bodily control. Tremors, falls, loss of vision—these and more are the debilitating symptoms of MS. There is no cure and few sure treatments. About half the people who develop MS eventually die of complications from the disease. It is no wonder then that various studies have found an elevated risk of suicide among MS patients.

Most, however, desperately try to find ways to cope. Their search leads MS patients to try a wide range of therapies, in both mainstream and alternative medicine. Passionate arguments take place daily about the effectiveness of this or that method. One reason for so much uncertainty about the effectiveness of the treatment is the mercurial behavior of the disease.

Multiple sclerosis is hard to diagnose and even harder to predict. Its many symptoms range from dizziness and fatigue to highly specific and alarming developments such as temporary blindness.

## The Erratic Nature of MS

Once a diagnosis of MS has been made, a major task remains. That is to determine what form of the disease the patient has. There are four major types, characterized by

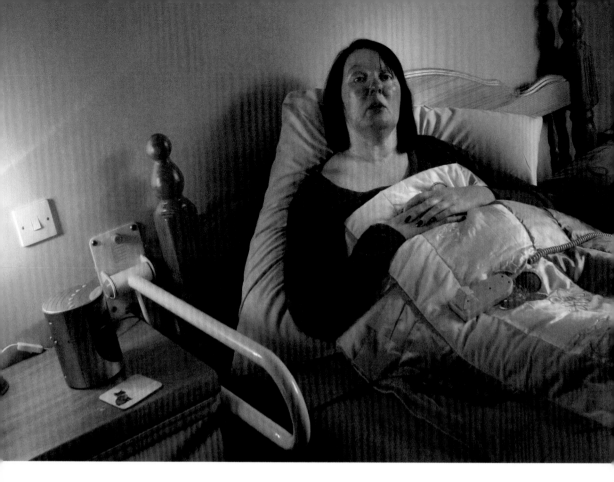

how steadily and rapidly the disease attacks the nervous system.

Primary progressive multiple sclerosis (PPMS) is a form of the disease in which it attacks and never lets up, though the patient's decline may be gradual. Some treatments seem to slow down the effects, but it is hard to be sure.

Secondary progressive multiple sclerosis (SPMS) is a version in which the disease begins sporadically, then takes hold and puts the patient into a steady decline.

The worst and rarest category is malignant MS, a form of the disease which advances like wildfire and kills victims within months. No treatments seem to be effective.

However, by far the most common form is known as relapsing remitting multiple sclerosis (RRMS). Attacks are repeatedly followed by natural remission (in which symptoms temporarily disappear). This can fool people into thinking a treatment has been effective. Conversely, when it suddenly reappears it can cause a person to wrongly blame a treatment or lifestyle for the change. Above all it contributes to a sense of helplessness.

## Patients Are Driven to Seek Alternatives

The standard treatments for MS aim to reduce inflammation and slow the loss of myelin, the fatty sheath that surrounds and protects the nerve fibers. Steroids, which are best known for ruining the lives of athletes, are a mainstream MS therapy. Apart from their uncertain effects, many patients complain of side effects, such as weight gain and high blood pressure. A thirty-one-year-old mom coping with MS writes in her journal: "With every illness, every treatment, every time in the hospital . . . I have gained weight. It does not seem to make a difference if I eat healthy. . . . For every step I make to become more healthy, something happens which only puts me back 3–4 steps (like being put on steroids). It seems like a vicious cycle that never ends."

Like many frustrated MS patients, this woman chooses to put her faith in an alternative therapy. In her case it is a completely benign activity:

> I have come up with a goal that I think will help. I recently learned of the MS Challenge Walk. . . . It will take a lot of training in order for me to be ready to do this. It is walking 50 miles over 3 days. . . . I don't expect results overnight. To do that would mean that I would not really be healthy. True change, becoming healthy takes a long time. . . . It is a matter of creating a different lifestyle. That is my goal.[2]

Other MS patients go in for much riskier alternative treatments. A man named Brad developed MS shortly after he quit smoking. Suspecting a possible connection, he began to use a nicotine patch as therapy. He believes it helped slow the disease for several years, and he may be right. Some evidence from animal studies suggests that nicotine may have a positive effect on MS. However, nicotine usage has many risks as well.

Ironically, smokers are twice as likely as nonsmokers to contract MS in the first place. Whether that is from the nicotine or one of the thousands of other chemicals in cigarettes is unknown, but it is certain that nicotine weakens blood vessels and contributes to heart disease and stroke.

Nicotine patches are far safer than smoking (which introduces thousands of other volatile chemicals into the body), but even nicotine introduced via a transdermal patch poses risks. Recent research indicates that as nicotine breaks down in the body, it produces other chemicals that can interfere with natural processes as well as medicines a person may be taking.

Some people believe that smoking or ingesting marijuana helps control the muscle spasms that MS causes. Medical researchers have not been able to establish clear evidence one way or the other. Like tobacco, marijuana poses health hazards along with any putative benefit. It also carries a special risk: In most places its use even for medical purposes is outlawed.

One more risk of alternative therapies deserves mention. Some alternative therapies can be extremely costly, and most are not covered by health insurance. As an investigative reporter, Ellen Burstein McFarland was not prone to falling for a fast sales pitch. But when she came down with MS, panic clouded her judgment. She became convinced that a questionable therapy called Superesonant Wavenergy could cure her. It was all the more convincing because it was being promoted by Irving I. Dardik, a respected vascular surgeon and former head of the Olympic Committee's Sports Medicine Council.

His credentials proved no barrier to fraud. MacFarland recalls:

> I believed Dardik's enthusiastic assertion that he had the answer to MS. He emphasized he was not talking about a remission; he could cure me. It would take a year and I would walk again. My family gave in to my plea to pay this man $100,000–$50,000 of it up front. Within seven months, my condition deteriorated. Dr. Irving I. Dardik's worthless cure and greed had taken a year of my life that I could not afford to lose. I had to quit my job, I needed 24-hour nursing care, and I now used a wheelchair full-time. Dardik offered no restitution.[3]

Research has shown that smokers are twice as likely to contract multiple sclerosis as nonsmokers. (© **SuperStock Inc./ SuperStock**)

Dardik was later stripped of his medical license and fined, but there is no shortage of greedy individuals ready to take his place. Most experts do not rule out alternative therapies for MS, but they urge patients to focus on those that are benign, such as exercise or massage, or fairly certain to be harmless and relatively inexpensive, such as acupuncture.

## Mainstream Research Continues

In the meantime, evidence-based medical research on MS is progressing. Evidence-based research involves large numbers of participants in controlled tests where neither the experimenters nor the participants know whether they are getting treatment or a placebo. Such trials (as they are known) have established that certain drugs are effective in slowing the course of the disease.

An individual patient can never be sure whether a particular treatment is helping, hurting, or having no effect at all. By engaging thousands of patients in studies designed to screen out false hopes or expectations, medical science can perhaps discover both causes and reliable treatments for this cruel and capricious disease.

### Notes

1. Joan Carter, "My Experience with the Monster," All About Multiple Sclerosis, August 6, 2001. www.multsclerosis.org/joanssstory.html.
2. "Jamie," "My MS Journal," April 19, 2008. http://mymsjournal.blogspot.com.
3. Virginia Foster and Ellen Burstein MacFarland, "Clear Thinking About Alternative Therapies," National MS Society, 2008. www.nationalmssociety.org/download.aspx?id=72.

# CHAPTER 1

# Understanding Multiple Sclerosis

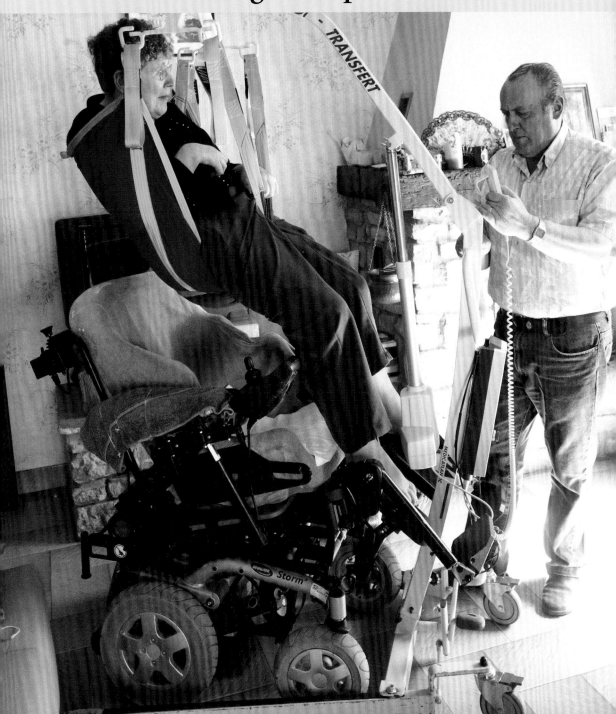

# Overview of Multiple Sclerosis

### Ruthan Brodsky

Multiple sclerosis is a feared but widely misunderstood disease. In the following viewpoint writer Ruthan Brodsky defines and describes the malady. It is, she says, an autoimmune disease, meaning that it results from the body's immune system mistakenly attacking itself. In the case of multiple sclerosis, it is the protective jacket around nerve cells that bears the attack. Exactly why this happens is a mystery. Brodsky lists some possible causes, including a sneaky virus that may be hiding in some nerve cells. A cure has also proven elusive, but some drug treatments are available to try to slow the disease or mitigate its symptoms. Brodsky is a health and medical writer based in Michigan.

*Photo on previous page.* A husband helps his wife, who suffers from MS, to transfer from bed to wheelchair. MS sufferers face an uphill task in living with the diseases. (Phanie/Photo Researchers, Inc.)

Multiple sclerosis (MS) is a chronic autoimmune disorder affecting movement, sensation, and bodily functions. It is caused by destruction of the myelin insulation covering nerve fibers (neurons) in the central nervous system (brain and spinal cord).

**SOURCE:** Ruthan Brodsky, *Gale Encyclopedia of Medicine*. Detroit: Gale, 2006. Copyright © 2006 Gale, Cengage Learning. Reproduced by permission of Gale, a part of Cengage Learning.

## Description

MS is a nerve disorder caused by destruction of the insulating layer surrounding neurons in the brain and spinal cord. This insulation, called myelin, helps electrical signals pass quickly and smoothly between the brain and the rest of the body. When the myelin is destroyed, nerve messages are sent more slowly and less efficiently. Patches of scar tissue, called plaques, form over the affected areas, further disrupting nerve communication. The

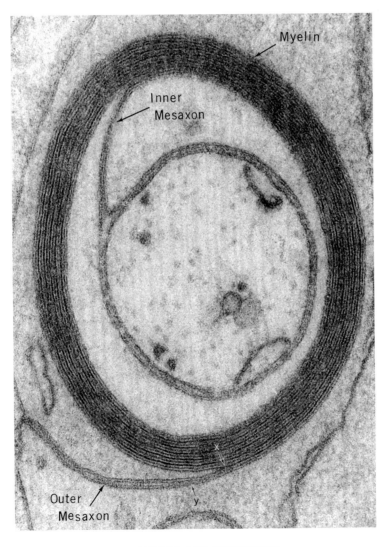

Multiple sclerosis, a chronic autoimmune disorder, is caused by destruction of the myelin sheath, an insulating layer that surrounds nerves in the brain and spinal cord. (**Don W. Fawcett/ Photo Researchers, Inc.**)

symptoms of MS occur when the brain and spinal cord nerves no longer communicate properly with other parts of the body. MS causes a wide variety of symptoms and can affect vision, balance, strength, sensation, coordination, and bodily functions.

Multiple sclerosis affects more than a quarter of a million people in the United States. Most people have their first symptoms between the ages of 20 and 40; symptoms rarely begin before 15 or after 60. Women are almost twice as likely to get MS as men, especially in their early years. People of northern European heritage are more likely to be affected than people of other racial backgrounds, and MS rates are higher in the United States, Canada, and northern Europe than in other parts of the world. MS is very rare among Asians, North and South American Indians, and Eskimos.

## Attacked by the Immune System

Multiple sclerosis is an autoimmune disease, meaning its cause is an attack by the body's own immune system. For unknown reasons, immune cells attack and destroy the myelin sheath that insulates neurons in the brain and spinal cord. This myelin sheath, created by other brain cells called glia, speeds transmission and prevents electrical activity in one cell from short-circuiting to another cell. Disruption of communication between the brain and other parts of the body prevent normal passage of sensations and control messages, leading to the symptoms of MS. The demyelinated areas appear as plaques, small round areas of gray neuron without the white myelin covering. The progression of symptoms in MS is correlated with development of new plaques in the portion of the brain or spinal cord controlling the affected areas. Because there appears to be no pattern in the appearance of new plaques, the progression of MS can be unpredictable.

Despite considerable research, the trigger for this autoimmune destruction is still unknown. At various times, evidence has pointed to genes, environmental factors, viruses, or a combination of these.

The risk of developing MS is higher if another family member is affected, suggesting the influence of genetic factors. In addition, the higher prevalence of MS among people of northern European background suggests some genetic susceptibility.

The role of an environmental factor is suggested by studies of the effect of migration on the risk of developing MS. Age plays an important role in determining this change in risk—young people in low-risk groups who move into countries with higher MS rates display the risk rates of their new surroundings, while older migrants retain the risk of their original home country. One interpretation of these studies is that an environmental factor, either protective or harmful, is acquired in early life; the risk of disease later in life reflects the effects of the early environment.

These same data can be used to support the involvement of a slow-acting virus, one that is acquired early on but begins its destructive effects much later. Slow viruses are known to cause other diseases, including AIDS. In addition, viruses have been implicated in other autoimmune diseases. Many claims have been made for the role of viruses, slow or otherwise, as the trigger for MS, but as of 2001 no strong candidate has emerged.

How a virus could trigger the autoimmune reaction is also unclear. There are two main models of virally induced autoimmunity. The first suggests the immune system is actually attacking a virus (one too well-hidden for detection in the laboratory), and the myelin damage is an unintentional consequence of fighting the infection. The second model suggests the immune system mistakes myelin for a viral protein, one it encountered during a prior infection. Primed for the attack, it destroys myelin because it resembles the previously recognized viral invader.

# MS Strips Away Myelin Sheath

Multiple sclerosis (MS) is an autoimmune disease in which immune cells attack and destroy the myelin sheath that stimulates neurons in the brain and spinal cord. When the myelin is destroyed, nerve messages are sent more slowly and less efficiently. Scar tissue then forms over the affected areas, disrupting nerve communication. MS symptoms occur when the brain and spinal cord nerves cease to communicate properly with other parts of the body.

Myelin sheath

Absence of myelin sheath

Nerve cell

Taken from: Illustration by Electronic Illustrators Group.

Either of these models allows a role for genetic factors, since certain genes can increase the likelihood of autoimmunity. Environmental factors as well might change the sensitivity of the immune system or interact with myelin to provide the trigger for the secondary immune response. Possible environmental triggers that have been invoked in MS include viral infection, trauma, electrical injury, and chemical exposure, although controlled studies do not support a causative role. . . .

## Symptoms

Weakness in one or both legs is common, and may be the first symptom noticed by a person with MS. Muscle spasticity, or excessive tightness, is also common and may be more disabling than weakness.

Double vision or eye tremor may result from involvement of the nerve pathways controlling movement of the eye muscles. Visual disturbances result from involvement of the optic nerves (optic neuritis) and may include development of blind spots in one or both eyes, changes in color vision, or blindness. Optic neuritis usually involves only one eye at a time and is often associated with movement of the affected eye.

More than half of all people affected by MS have pain during the course of their disease, and many experience chronic pain, including pain from spasticity. Acute pain occurs in about 10% of cases. This pain may be a sharp, stabbing pain especially in the face, neck, or down the back. Facial numbness and weakness are also common.

Cognitive changes, including memory disturbances, depression, and personality changes, are found in people affected by MS, though it is not entirely clear whether these changes are due primarily to the disease or to the psychological reaction to it. Depression may be severe enough to require treatment in up to 25% of those with MS. A smaller number of people experience disease-related euphoria, or abnormally elevated mood, usually after a long disease duration and in combination with other psychological changes.

Symptoms of MS may be worsened by heat or increased body temperature, including fever, intense physical activity, or exposure to sun, hot baths or showers.

## Diagnosis

There is no single test that confirms the diagnosis of multiple sclerosis, and there are a number of other diseases with similar symptoms. While one person's diagnosis may be immediately suggested by her symptoms and history, another's may not be confirmed without multiple tests and prolonged observation. The distribution of symptoms is important: MS affects multiple areas of the body over time. The pattern of symptoms is also critical, especially evidence of the relapsing-remitting pattern, so a detailed medical history is one of the most important parts of the diagnostic process. A thorough search to exclude other causes of a patient's symptoms is especially important if the following features are present: 1) family history of neurologic disease, 2) symptoms and findings attributable to a single anatomic location, 3) persistent back pain, 4) age of onset over 60 or under 15 years of age, or 5) progressively worsening disease.

In addition to the medical history and a standard neurological exam, several lab tests are used to help confirm or rule out a diagnosis of MS:

- Magnetic resonance imaging (MRI) can reveal plaques on the brain and spinal cord. Gadolinium enhancement can distinguish between old and new plaques, allowing a correlation of new plaques with new symptoms. Plaques may be seen in several other diseases as well, including encephalomyelitis, neurosarcoidosis, and cerebral lupus. Plaques on MRI may be difficult to distinguish from small strokes, areas of decreased blood flow, or changes seen with trauma or normal aging.

- A lumbar puncture, or spinal tap, is done to measure levels of immune proteins, which are usually elevated in the cerebrospinal fluid of a person with MS. This test may not be necessary if other tests are diagnostic.

- Evoked potential tests, electrical tests of conduction speed in the nerves, can reveal reduced speeds consistent with the damage caused by plaques. These tests may be done with small electrical charges applied to the skin (somatosensory evoked potential), with light patterns flashed on the eyes (visual evoked potential), or with sounds presented to the ears (auditory evoked potential). . . .

## Treatment

The three major drugs previously approved for the treatment of MS affect the course of the disease. None of these drugs is a cure, but they can slow disease progression in many patients. . . .

Although the . . . drugs stop relapses and may keep patients in relatively good health for the short-term, their long-term success has not been proven, and they don't work well for patients who have reached a steadily progressive stage of MS. In the meantime, new approaches to using current therapies are being researched especially using a combination of different types of agents when one agent alone is not effective. . . .

## Prognosis

It is difficult to predict how multiple sclerosis will progress in any one person. Most people with MS will be able to continue to walk and function at their work for many years after their diagnosis. The factors associated with the mildest course of MS are being female, having the relapsing-remitting form, having the first symptoms at a younger age, having longer periods of remission between relapses, and initial symptoms of decreased sensation or vision rather than of weakness or incoordination.

Less than 5% of people with MS have a severe progressive form, leading to death from complications within five years. At the other extreme, 10–20% have a benign form, with a very slow or no progression of their symptoms. The most recent studies show that about seven out of 10 people with MS are still alive 25 years after their diagnosis, compared to about nine out of 10 people of similar age without disease. On average, MS shortens the lives of affected women by about six years, and men by 11 years. Suicide is a significant cause of death in MS, especially in younger patients.

The degree of disability a person experiences five years after onset is, on average, about three-quarters of the expected disability at 10–15 years. A benign course for the first five years usually indicates the disease will not cause marked disability.

There is no known way to prevent multiple sclerosis. Until the cause of the disease is discovered, this is unlikely to change. Good nutrition; adequate rest; avoidance of stress, heat, and extreme physical exertion; and good bladder hygiene may improve quality of life and reduce symptoms.

# The Causes of Multiple Sclerosis

## Harvey Simon

The key to curing a disease is to understand what its causes are. In the following viewpoint medical educator Harvey Simon describes the effort to pin down the causes of multiple sclerosis (MS). The mechanism of MS is well understood—the body's immune system mistakenly attacks the myelin that sheathes nerve cells. However, Simon explains, the reason that this happens remains a mystery. It may be that a combination of factors, such as genetic predisposition, viral infection, and possibly even a certain kind of vaccination, come into play. If, as many researchers suspect, viruses do play a role in triggering MS, the question of which virus is responsible has yet to be answered. Simon is an associate professor of medicine at Harvard Medical School and founding editor of the *Harvard Men's Health Watch*.

The cause, or causes, of multiple sclerosis [MS] remains a mystery. Genetic factors certainly play a role in MS. No single gene, however, is likely to be responsible for causing MS. Rather, the current theory is that the disease occurs in people with a genetic suscepti- bility who are exposed to some environmental assault (a virus or a toxin) that disrupts the blood-brain barrier. Immune factors converge in the nerve cells and trigger inflammation and an autoimmune attack (a self-attack) on myelin and axons [nerve cell branches]. Still, a num- ber of disease patterns have been observed in patients, and some experts believe that MS may prove to be not a single disorder, but may represent several diseases with different causes.

Some research suggests that all autoimmune diseases are basically due to the same genetic error. A 2001 study found, for example, that the T-cell immune factors in

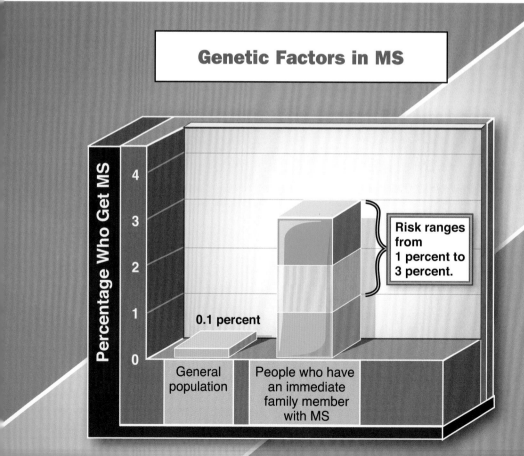

Genetic Factors in MS

Risk ranges from 1 percent to 3 percent.

0.1 percent

General population

People who have an immediate family member with MS

Percentage Who Get MS

Taken from: Arthur Schoenstadt, "Multiple Sclerosis Causes," e-MedTV, July 15, 2006.

type 1 diabetes target the same self-antigens as in multiple sclerosis (MS). Many questions are unanswered, however. It is not known why the diseases develop in different locations to cause separate disorders. Nor, why some autoimmune events occur in everyone but not everyone develops an autoimmune disease.

## Genetic Factors

Genetic factors probably play some role in making a person susceptible to the disease process leading to multiple sclerosis. In particular, abnormalities in the human leukocyte antigen (HLA) region located on chromosome 6 appear to be more prevalent among people with MS. Researchers theorize, however, that a combination of genes (not a single gene) is implicated in the development of MS, and the risk for someone inheriting all of these genetic factors is less than 5%. Advanced techniques called microarray technologies are now making it possible to scan hundreds of genes and identify those most likely to be contributors to MS. Genetic research may also pave the way for the development of new drugs to treat this disease. For example, researchers have recently identified the Olig1 gene as a key regulator in repairing damaged myelin-producing cells.

## Infectious Organisms

Infectious organisms, most likely viruses, are the top suspects for triggering the autoimmune response in people genetically susceptible to MS. There are a number of reasons for this belief:

- The geographical distribution of the disease. The number of MS cases increases the further one gets from the equator in either direction.
- Multiple sclerosis clusters. Four separate clusters of multiple sclerosis outbreaks occurred between 1943 and 1989 in the Faroe Islands, located between Iceland and Scandinavia. During World War II, this

## FAST FACT

According to the U.S. Centers for Disease Control and Prevention, a review of all available scientific evidence does not support the suggestion that hepatitis B vaccine causes or worsens MS.

region was occupied by British troops. The incidence of MS increased each year for 20 years after the war, leading some researchers to think that the troops might have brought with them some disease-causing organism. In fact, one theory suggests that these findings offer evidence that MS is a sexually transmitted infection that occurs during adolescence. For example, the disease clusters observed in the Faroe Islands could be related to high sexual activity between the troops and local young women. A high incidence of MS is found in countries with a high degree of sexual permissiveness. MS is also very rare in traditional cultures, but increases in people from these regions when they immigrate to industrialized Western nations.

- Viral similarity to myelin. Some viruses are strikingly similar to the myelin protein and may therefore cause confusion in the immune system, causing the T cells to continue to attack their own protein rather than the viral antigen. More than one antigen may be involved; some may trigger the disease, and others may keep the process going.

### Prime Suspects

Although many infectious microorganisms have been investigated, no one organism has emerged as a proven trigger. It is possible different patients may be affected by different organisms, and that infections cause some, but not all, cases of MS. Organisms that are at the top of the suspect list are those that can affect the central nervous system. The following are three primary suspects:

- HHV-6. Herpesvirus 6 (a form of herpesvirus that causes roseola, a benign disease in children) is also known to cause encephalitis (brain inflammation) in patients with impaired immune systems. A number of studies have reported higher than normal rates of HHV-6 infection in patients, and some experts believe that may be important in MS. Other experts argue, however, that nearly everyone harbors this virus and there is still no evidence of a causal relationship. Other herpes viruses can also infect brain cells. They include herpes simplex 1 and 2 (the causes of oral and genital herpes), varicella-zoster virus (the cause of chicken pox and shingles), and cytomegalovirus.

- Epstein-Barr virus (EBV). Evidence suggests an association between EBV, the cause of mononucleosis, and MS. EBV is an extremely common virus and

The Epstein-Barr virus (EBV), shown in this colored electron micrograph, is seen as circles with inner colored regions of DNA (nucleic acid). High levels of EBV may pose a risk of developing MS. (**Dr. Gopel Murti/ Photo Researchers, Inc.**)

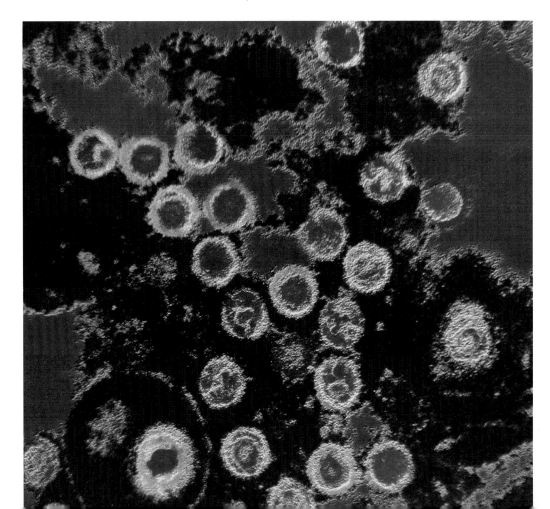

another member of the herpes virus family. Nearly all people have been exposed to EBV. However, researchers have discovered that people who are especially sensitive to the virus and have unusually high levels of EBV antibodies may have a greater risk of developing MS. Scientists are still uncertain if EBV is a cause of MS. EBV has also been linked to other autoimmune diseases such as lupus.

- *Chlamydia Pneumoniae.* This atypical bacterium has been associated with persistent inflammation. A few studies have reported significantly higher rates of previous *Chlamydia* infection in patients with MS than in individuals without MS. An important group of 2000 studies reported no connection at all between *Chlamydia* and MS, and many experts now believe there is no strong evidence linking the microbe to MS. It is still possible, however, that the infection, which can cause widespread inflammation, plays a role early in the course of the disease in some individuals.

Other viruses that have been investigated include measles virus, adenovirus, and the retroviruses (HIV, HTLV-I, and HTLV-II), but none have emerged as having any importance.

## Hepatitis Vaccine Questioned

Concerns about a link between the hepatitis B vaccine and MS led France to halt a major vaccination program in 1998. Subsequent research investigating whether the hepatitis B vaccine is indeed associated with an increased risk of MS has yielded mixed results. It appears that the vaccine would be, at most, a contributing—but not the sole—factor in MS development. At present, the evidence has not warranted any change in American immunization policies. Research has ruled out a link between any other vaccinations, such as for influenza or tetanus, and relapses of MS.

# The Symptoms of Multiple Sclerosis

**John Richert**

The list of symptoms of multiple sclerosis is staggering. Many of them are elusive. They come and go. They may or may not be causally related to MS. In the following viewpoint physician John Richert discusses the difficulty of pinning down symptoms and whether various treatments are effective in suppressing them. Symptoms such as pain, exhaustion, hypersensitivity to heat, and tingling sensations are subjective. That does not mean they are not real, but as Richert notes, it does mean that they are impossible for the clinician to measure objectively. This makes evaluating various treatments very difficult. The placebo effect—a psychological boost in the feeling of well-being that follows a treatment regardless of its physical effect—often comes into play. Richert says experience shows that the placebo effect wears off before long and warns that the cost and risk of some alternative therapies make them an unwise choice. Richert is the executive vice president of research and clinical programs at the National Multiple Sclerosis Society.

**SOURCE:** John Richert, "What We Are Doing About Symptoms That Can't Be Measured Easily," *Inside MS*, vol. 25, February–March 2007, pp. 41–43. Copyright © 2007 National Multiple Sclerosis Society. Reproduced by permission.

P ain. Fatigue. Mood alterations. Pins-and-needles sensations. These are common and often disabling effects of MS [multiple sclerosis]. Indeed, they are complex symptoms that need to be treated.

We often hear from people with MS that the treatments recommended by their doctors are not providing adequate relief. As a result, many alternative therapies are espoused by people both inside and outside established medical circles.

Bee stings. Marijuana. Low-dose naltrexone. Vitamin $B_{12}$. Desensitization related to potential allergens. Dietary changes. Antibiotics. All of these, and many others, have been recommended for the treatment of MS symptoms—with limited scientific evidence to back them up. What should we be doing about it?

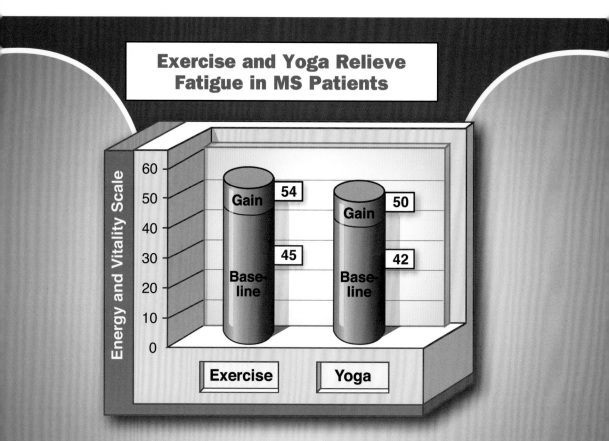

**Exercise and Yoga Relieve Fatigue in MS Patients**

Taken from: B.S. Oken et al., "Randomized Controlled Trial of Yoga and Exercise in Multiple Sclerosis," *Neurology*, June 8, 2004.

The National MS Society is often asked to advocate for unproven treatments for MS symptoms, precisely because the symptoms are so troubling and the available conventional treatments fail to provide adequate relief for many. But, instead of giving advice based on insufficient knowledge, we must acquire the knowledge we lack. Our priorities must be to learn how to evaluate convincingly the therapeutic potential of any treatment that might relieve troubling and disabling MS symptoms.

## Subtle Symptoms

The symptoms that are the subject of this article have one thing in common: They are difficult or nearly impossible to measure objectively at the present time. They are largely felt—not seen—and a health-care provider or a researcher is unable to gauge their severity through observation. We have to rely on what our patients tell us. And since individuals are certain to describe their feelings differently, researchers have a problem.

In order to prove that a treatment is effective, researchers need to measure the beneficial effects of that treatment by a uniform standard.

The National MS Society is beginning to address the question of how to evaluate symptoms for which we currently lack good objective measures. The goal is to help researchers devise ways to measure "unmeasurable" symptoms so that clinical studies can be designed that reliably answer questions about efficacy. This is the only way we will be able to make recommendations based on data rather than on hope or opinion.

## The Placebo Effect

These issues have been with us for a long time. Fifteen years ago many of my patients reported to me that bee stings improved their energy levels, lessened spasticity, and lifted their mood. I had no objection to people subjecting themselves to bee sting treatments if they were not allergic to bee venom. Dozens of my patients tried it. However, all but two eventually abandoned it because the beneficial effects quickly disappeared.

Most of the people who reported a brief benefit after receiving bee stings were almost certainly experiencing a placebo effect, which is an entirely normal phenomenon. The human system often responds to hope and positive expectations by producing some relief.

It's not necessarily important to distinguish between a placebo effect and the more robust, physiologic response if we are dealing with a benign form of treatment. Even brief relief is, after all, a good thing. So over the years, my advice about alternatives that have been neither proven nor unproven (due to lack of adequate study) hasn't changed: "If it's safe, and it doesn't break the bank, and you don't choose an alternative treatment to the exclusion of therapies of proven value, I have no objections."

The issue becomes problematic with unproven alternatives that do carry degrees of risk. . . . Alternative treatments that have abuse potential add a particularly vexing dimension to the problem. When a drug or substance is legally available only for medical purposes, a doctor can be faced with having to decide which people need the treatment for medical reasons and which ones simply want a way to obtain the drug.

## FAST FACT

At some point, up to 40 percent of people with MS suffer an attack of optic neuritis.

## Marijuana Merits Study

Because marijuana has been described as having therapeutic value for some of the symptoms that are so difficult to measure objectively, and because its study has suffered from the problems that we are discussing here, the National MS Society has convened a special task force to evaluate all of the current evidence for the efficacy of marijuana for MS symptoms, and all the evidence relat-

The National Multiple Sclerosis Society has convened a special task force to evaluate the current evidence on marijuana's efficacy in treating MS symptoms. (**Guido Benschop/Reuters/ Landov**)

ing to adverse effects. The task force will then determine if an appropriate risk-benefit analysis can be conducted or, alternatively, what additional research studies are needed to answer the open questions. If a drug with abuse potential is convincingly shown to have therapeutic benefit that significantly outweighs its risks, we must have valid data to convince the legal authorities that its use is justified.

To increase available data, we have already initiated funding of our first grant to study the effects of cannabis on MS-related spasticity. This trial is going forward thanks in no small part to improved methods for objectively measuring the severity of spasticity.

As a physician and as a leader in the National MS Society, I want you to know that we will follow what the best data tell us, pursue ways to acquire more knowledge, and push to make all treatments proven to be effective available to all who need them.

# How Multiple Sclerosis Is Diagnosed

## National Multiple Sclerosis Society

In the following viewpoint the National Multiple Sclerosis Society explains the complexities of diagnosing the disease for which it is named. First, the range of symptoms associated with multiple sclerosis is staggering. No one symptom is definitive. Furthermore, no single test can identify someone as a victim of the disease. However, a doctor who suspects MS can look for a number of indicators, and several kinds of scans can assist in confirming a diagnosis. Unfortunately, the same symptoms and signs can have other causes, so making a positive diagnosis of MS can be a lengthy process. The National Multiple Sclerosis Society is a nonprofit network that helps people affected by MS by funding cutting-edge research, driving change through advocacy, facilitating professional education, and providing programs and services that help people with MS and their families move their lives forward.

**SOURCE:** National Multiple Sclerosis Society, "Multiple Sclerosis Basic Facts Series: Diagnosis," nationalmssociety.org, 2008. Reproduced by permission.

In MS [multiple sclerosis], myelin is lost in multiple areas, leaving scar tissue called sclerosis. These damaged areas are also known as plaques or lesions. Sometimes the underlying nerve fiber (or axon) is also damaged or broken.

When myelin or the nerve fiber is destroyed or damaged, the ability of the nerves to conduct electrical impulses to and from the brain is disrupted, and this produces the various symptoms of MS. . . .

## No One Test

The diagnosis of MS can be very difficult. Because there is no single test that can be used to confirm MS, the process of diagnosis typically involves:

- evidence from the person's history
- a clinical examination
- and one or more laboratory tests.

A physician often requires all three in order to rule out other possible causes for symptoms and to gather facts consistent with a diagnosis of MS.

## Symptoms

The range of symptoms experienced by people with MS varies dramatically from person to person. Symptoms are problems that are reported by the person him- or herself.

MS symptoms can include reduced or abnormal sensations, weakness, vision changes, clumsiness, sudden loss of bladder control, and so on. Symptoms might appear in any combination and be mild or severe. They are usually experienced for unpredictable periods of time.

But symptoms alone don't indicate MS. Any one or combination of these symptoms might have causes unrelated to MS.

After taking a careful medical history, including all of a person's symptoms, past and present, the physician will

# MS Symptoms Often Come and Go

In about 85 percent of people with MS, relapses occur—meaning that old symptoms get worse or that new symptoms appear. Although relapses may be followed by periods in which the disease goes into remission, the effects of MS are cumulative over time.

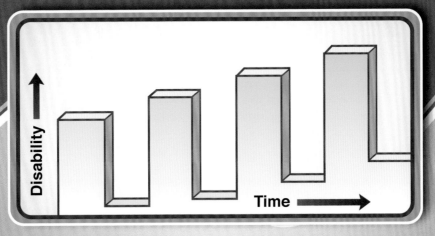

Taken from: MS Lifelines, "Types of MS," EMD Serano, 2008.

do a series of tests to check for signs that can explain the symptoms or point to disease activity of which a person may not be aware.

Signs are indications of the disease that are objectively determined by a physician. Some signs might even explain a person's symptoms, but others have no corresponding symptom.

## Certain Indicators

Common signs that can be detected by the doctor during a physical examination include:

- altered eye movements and abnormal responses of the pupils
- subtle changes in speech patterns
- altered reflex responses
- impaired coordination

- sensory disturbances
- evidence of spasticity and/or weakness in the arms or legs.

## Bodily Tests

The physical examination may consist of the following:

- an eye examination, which may reveal the presence of damage to the optic nerve

A physical examination can detect altered eye movement, abnormal pupil response, altered reflex responses, and impaired coordination —all common symptoms indicating possible MS. (© The Stock Asylum, LLC/ Alamy)

- a check of muscle strength, by gently but firmly pulling and pushing a person's arms and legs
- measuring coordination, usually with a finger-to-nose test, in which a person is asked to bring the tip of an index finger to the nose rapidly, with eyes open and then closed
- an examination of body surface sensation, tested with a safety pin, and by a feather or a light touch
- a test of vibratory sense, with a vibrating tuning fork placed against a joint or bone so the person experiences a buzz-like sensation
- a test of reflexes, using fingers or a small rubber mallet.

## MRI Scan

Laboratory tests may be the crucial element of the diagnosis process. The preferred test, which detects plaques or scarring possibly caused by MS, is magnetic resonance imaging (MRI).

The MRI scan is a diagnostic tool that currently offers the most sensitive non-invasive way of imaging the brain.

Unlike Computerized Tomography (CT) or conventional X-ray, the MRI scan does not use radiation. Instead, it uses magnetism and radio waves. Powerful magnetic fields interact with the hydrogen atoms found in the water contained in all body tissues and fluids. Radio frequency signals cause these hydrogen atoms to release energy, and computers translate the changes into cross-sectional images.

The scanning procedure is very sensitive and can often create pictures of lesions or areas of damage that would be missed by a CT scan.

Although the absence of radiation is an asset, the powerful magnetic field of MRI means that it can't be used by people who have cardiac pacemakers or metal implants, such as aneurysm clips, in their bodies. Dental fillings cause no problem.

<br>

## FAST FACT

According to WebMD, up to 10 percent of people diagnosed with multiple sclerosis actually have some other condition that mimics MS.

An abnormal MRI does not necessarily mean MS. There are other diseases that cause lesions in the brain that look like those caused by MS. There are also spots found in healthy individuals, particularly in older persons, which are not related to any ongoing disease process. These are often called UBOs, for unidentified bright objects.

On the other hand, a normal MRI does not absolutely rule out MS. About 5% of people, who are confirmed to have MS on the basis of other criteria, do not show any lesions in the brain on MRI. These people may have lesions in the spinal cord or may have lesions that cannot be detected by MRI.

A clear-cut diagnosis might be made based on an evaluation of symptoms, signs, and the results of an MRI, but additional tests may be ordered as well. These include tests of evoked potential, cerebrospinal fluid, and blood.

### Evoked Potential

Evoked potential (EP) tests are electrical diagnostic studies that can show if there is a slowing of messages in various parts of the brain. They often provide evidence of scarring along nerve pathways not apparent any other way.

The EP test most widely accepted as an aid to an MS diagnosis is the Visual Evoked Potential (VEP). The person sits before a screen on which an alternating checkerboard pattern is displayed.

The results are interpreted by a neurologist or neurophysiologist who has special training in this test.

### Spinal Fluid Test

Cerebrospinal fluid, sampled by a lumbar puncture (also called a spinal tap), is tested for levels of certain immune system proteins and for the presence of a staining pattern of antibodies called oligoclonal bands. These bands indicate an immune response within the central nervous system.

Oligoclonal bands are found in the spinal fluid of 90–95% of people with MS. However, they are present in other diseases as well, so oligoclonal bands alone cannot be relied on as positive proof of MS.

While there is no definitive blood test for MS, blood tests can positively rule out other causes for various neurologic symptoms such as Lyme disease, a group of diseases known as "collagen-vascular diseases," certain rare hereditary disorders, and AIDS.

## Two-Part Diagnosis

The basic "rule" for diagnosing MS requires both of the following:

1. Objective evidence of at least two areas of myelin loss, or demyelinating lesions, "separated in time and space." This means lesions have occurred in different places within the brain, spinal cord, or optic nerve at different points in time.

2. All other diseases that can cause similar neurologic symptoms have been objectively ruled out.

Until "1" and "2" have been satisfied, a physician will not be able to make a definite diagnosis of MS. Waiting in limbo is extremely trying. Receiving an incorrect diagnosis may be even worse.

# Treatments for Multiple Sclerosis

## Nicola O'Connell

The main form of treatment for MS is currently drug therapy. In the following viewpoint Nicola O'Connell describes the major drugs in use and their applications. While proven to have some benefits, they are not cures for the disease, and in some cases patients develop antibodies to the drugs themselves, blocking their beneficial effects. Therefore, researchers are testing new drugs to see if they will prove safer and more effective. O'Connell reports that the biggest hope lies in the development of stem cell therapy, which many scientists believe has the potential to reverse some of the damage caused by MS. O'Connell is an editor and writer who specializes in health care and medical issues, among other topics. She lives in London.

Traditionally treatment for multiple sclerosis (MS) focused on symptomatic relief, but disease-modifying therapies (DMTs), introduced a decade ago [ca. 1997], have helped to transform treatment. DMTs

**SOURCE:** Nicola O'Connell, "Pharmacy Update—Multiple Sclerosis, Part Two," *Chemist+Druggist*, January 20, 2007, p. 19. Copyright 2007 CMP Information Ltd. Reproduced by permission.

reduce the number and severity of relapses and ensure that continuing relapses are less severe and of shorter duration than previously experienced. All DMTs are self-injected under the skin or into a muscle.

## Three Drug Therapies

The first DMT, interferon beta-1b (Betaferon) was launched in the UK [United Kingdom] in 1995, followed by interferon beta-1a (Avonex and Rebif), and then glatiramer acetate (Copaxone). All three interferons inhibit the action of gamma-interferon and induce substances that suppress immune activity in the body.

Glatiramer acetate has a different mode of action. Specifically designed to treat MS, it is a synthetic protein

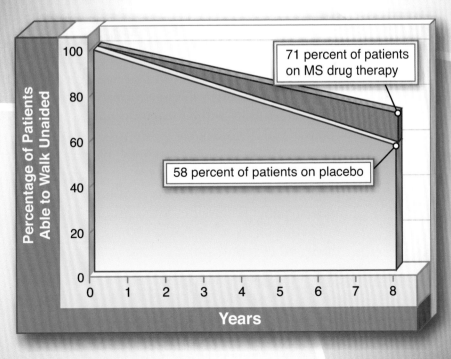

**Drug Therapy Delays Onset of Disability**

71 percent of patients on MS drug therapy

58 percent of patients on placebo

Percentage of Patients Able to Walk Unaided

Years

Taken from: R.A. Rudick et al., "Estimating Long-Term Effects of Disease-Modifying Drug Therapy in Multiple Sclerosis Patients," *Multiple Sclerosis*, vol. 11, no. 6, 2005.

composed of four major amino acids found in myelin (the basic protein in the sheath surrounding nerve fibres) and its action is based on this similarity to natural myelin.

In terms of efficacy, clinical data shows all three interferons and glatiramer acetate reduce frequency of relapse by an average of about 30 percent. Interferons cause temporary influenza-like adverse effects in 50 percent of patients. Glatiramer is generally much better tolerated, although some 15 percent of people experience transitory chest pain or tightness accompanied by anxiety and sweating. These symptoms are largely benign and typically only continue for up to 30 minutes.

DMTs are licensed for people with relapsing-remitting MS (RRMS). . . . For other types of MS, such as benign and primary progressive, treatment focuses on managing different symptoms. For example, amitriptyline may be used for burning and tingling pain, and gabapentin for trigeminal neuralgia and desmopressin for bladder problems. Corticosteroids, given orally or intravenously, are used to treat relapses. . . .

## Patients Develop Resistance

Evidence of the clinical significance of neutralising antibodies (NAbs) to interferon beta has recently emerged. As with most protein therapies, treatment with interferon beta can lead to the formation of binding antibodies (BAbs) and NAbs. NAbs prevent interferon beta from binding to its receptor, thereby blocking interferon-receptor activation, expression of interferon-inducible genes, and their biologic effects. Some 7 to 42 percent of treated patients develop NAbs against interferon beta, impacting on its effect. NAbs become detectable between three and 18 months after the start of treatment, with patients taking interferon beta-1b typically becoming positive earlier than those on interferon beta-1a.

In 2005 the European Federation of Neurological Societies (EFNS) published guidelines on anti-interferon beta antibody measurements. The guidelines state that while interferon beta is a first-line therapy for MS, NAbs are a major problem, and recommend patients taking interferon beta should be tested at 12 and 24 months. In NAb positive patients, measurements should be repeated as patients with low titres [quantities] frequently become NAb negative over time. Therapy should be discontinued in patients with high titres of NAbs sustained at repeated measurements with three- to six-month intervals.

> **FAST FACT**
>
> According to *E-Drug Digest*, some antidepressants help relieve certain MS symptoms, such as bowel spasms and incontinence.

"I would not advise patients who have antibodies to do nothing," says Dr Giovannoni, reader in neuroimmunology at the Institute of Neurology, University College, London, who has recently developed a new standardised assay for measuring NAbs. "Patients who are NAb positive and failing treatment can either switch to glatiramer acetate or, if their disease is more aggressive, mitoxantrone."

It is predicted that testing for NAbs will become routine. "Most centres are now testing for NAbs. In our centre, 20 to 25 percent of our patients have tested NAb positive," says Dr Tom Staunton, consultant neurologist at Norwich and Norfolk University Hospital. . . .

## New Drugs Emerging

Tysabri (natalizumab), licensed by the European Commission in June 2006, is the first in a new class of monoclonal antibody drugs for the treatment of MS. It is authorised for use as a DMT in people with highly active RRMS or rapidly evolving severe RRMS.

Tysabri appears to be promising: in a two-year clinical trial (AFFIRM) involving 942 patients, those treated with the drug experienced a 42 per cent reduced risk of progression of disability and a 68 per cent reduction of clinical relapses. When used in combination with interferon beta-1a in a trial involving 1,171 patients, the combination was shown to be significantly more effective than using interferon beta-1a alone.

However, safety concerns arose when the drug was associated with progressive multifocal leukoencephalopathy, a rare aggressive disorder of the nervous system. . . .

Cancer chemotherapy mitoxantrone is occasionally used to treat RRMS or secondary progressive MS where relapses are still a significant feature despite DMTs. The drug—not licensed for use in MS in the UK—was recently on trial at the Walton Centre for Neurology and Neurosurgery in Liverpool in a new treatment protocol for patients with very active RRMS. This new protocol uses mitoxantrone followed by glatiramer acetate as maintenance DMT. Following the success in reducing relapses and slowing disease progression shown in the small trial, a two-arm single blinded study is being initiated.

"We are moving into an era where we are looking at ways and means to combine current and emerging therapies to maximise patient benefits and minimise the

A multiple sclerosis patient receives an infusion of Tysabri, a new and controversial drug that appears to be promising in the fight against MS. (Gary Porter/MCT/ Landov)

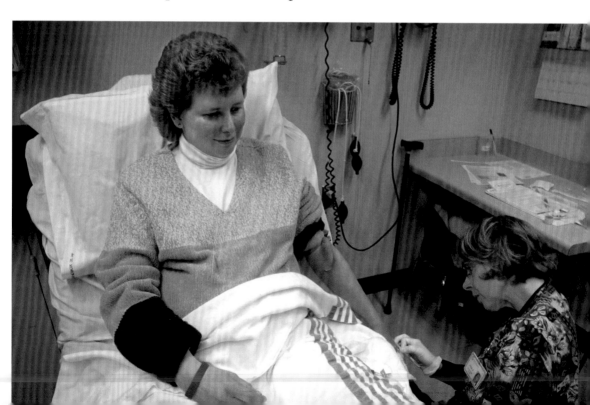

risk," says Dr [Mike] Boggild [consultant neurologist at the Walton Center], whose centre is leading the study. "Mitoxantrone suppresses quickly but cannot be used long-term, which is why we are examining this particular combination."

Campath (alemtuzumab) is another potential treatment for MS. Currently indicated for the treatment of B-cell chronic lymphocytic leukemia, it is undergoing trials to determine its potential in early MS. Campath is a monoclonal antibody, designed to target the part of the immune system involved in MS. The drug has nevertheless been associated with risks, including severe idiopathic thrombocytopenic purpura (a condition in which low blood platelet counts can lead to abnormal bleeding) and Grave's disease.

## Marijuana Treatment

The case for cannabis in MS has long been debated, but the cannabis-based mouth spray Sativex is now available in the UK on a [limited] basis. Manufacturer GW Pharmaceuticals has applied for a licence for the drug as a treatment for spasticity in people with MS. . . .

## Stem Cell Therapy

The other major development generating excitement is stem cell therapy. In theory, stem cells may be used to repair areas of damage. Potentially the stem cells could develop into nerve cells to repair damage to the brain, or develop into oligodendrocyctes to repair damage to the myelin. Their possible use is still many years away, as significant research is needed.

Says Dr Staunton: "Patients often ask about stem cell therapy but it is certainly not a tried and tested regimen and for clinical use it's very much an experimental tool. However, with the various treatments now being tested, I believe that within the next five to 10 years there will be a revolution in MS treatment."

# Emotional Dimensions of Multiple Sclerosis

## Nicholas LaRocca

In the viewpoint that follows, Nicholas LaRocca outlines the emotional toll inflicted by multiple sclerosis. The disease is exceptionally hard to accept, in part because there is no cure. Its unpredictable course—in some people, it strikes swift and hard, in most it comes and goes over many years—adds to the sense of helplessness that many patients experience. LaRocca lays out the stages of typical emotional responses to the disease and then goes on to describe some of the emotional changes that patients often undergo. Most people who contract MS learn to cope with it, he says, but inevitably the disease forces changes in lifestyle and emotional disposition. Fortunately, he indicates, the emotional toll can be mitigated with antidepressants and mood-stabilizing drugs. Nicholas LaRocca is a clinical psychologist who has studied multiple sclerosis for over twenty-seven years.

M S [multiple sclerosis] is a complex and unpredictable disease. Because no two people are psychologically identical, or experience MS in exactly the same way, each person's reaction to the disease will be unique. Although some of the early research in MS attempted to identify an "MS personality" that would predispose certain individuals to the disease or cause all people who have the disease to act in a certain way, it has been repeatedly demonstrated that no such personality type exists. A person's pre-MS personality, good or bad as it may be, is the same personality he or she will have after MS. And it is with this individual personality, and all its diverse traits, that a person will respond and react to the MS experience.

Some of the prior work in MS also described "stages" that people supposedly go through in their efforts to adjust to the disease. These "stage" models have typically been borrowed from cancer research and do not apply very well to chronic disease. MS is an uninvited and unwanted guest in people's lives that does not go away. As a result, the person with MS does not go through a definite, orderly set of stages culminating in adjustment. Rather, adjustment is an ongoing, lifelong process that ebbs and flows with the unpredictable changes brought about by the disease. Because each individual has a unique style and personal rhythm, which in large part determines how he or she will adjust, it is not particularly surprising that the process of adjustment seems to be more successful and comfortable for some than for others. Let us look at some of the emotional issues that arise as people try to incorporate MS into their lives.

## Uncertainty and Anxiety

Uncertainty and anxiety set in as soon as the first symptoms appear. MS can begin in a variety of ways, perhaps with a strange tingling sensation or numbness, sudden loss of vision, or unexplained weakness. Uncertainty surrounds these upsetting and unexplained symptoms. "Is it a brain tumor?" "Am I going crazy?" In some cases, the uncertainty drags on for some time until a diagnosis is finally established. Many people actually experience a brief sense of relief when the diagnosis of MS is confirmed. They are not happy about having the disease, but they are relieved to finally have an answer. In fact, in one study that looked at the diagnostic process in MS, the most anxious and unhappy patients following the diagnostic workup were those for whom no specific diagnosis could be confirmed.

Uncertainty does not evaporate with a confirmed diagnosis, however. Because the disease is unpredictable, people with MS are called upon to adjust to a lifetime of uncertainty about their health. They often do not know how they are going to feel or function tomorrow or next week, let alone several years down the road. In addition, there is uncertainty associated with the disease-modifying therapies that are recommended for relapsing forms of MS. These medications have been shown to reduce the number and severity of attacks and may slow disease progression; they are not, however, designed to reduce symptoms or make people feel better. Because of the way these medications function in the body, it is virtually impossible for any one individual to know the degree to which the disease-modifying medication is "working" at any given time. This much uncertainty can lead to a constant state of anxiety.

The effects of uncertainty and its attendant anxiety can include anger and irritability, indecision, difficulty in planning, feelings of helplessness, and pessimism about the future. Family members inevitably share in these feelings. As a result, all family members may find themselves looking

## FAST FACT

Although many multiple sclerosis sufferers believe that marijuana helps relieve their symptoms, a recent study suggests that its use by MS patients impairs thinking and is associated with depression and anxiety.

for "anchors"—ways to reduce uncertainty and increase a sense of security and stability within the household.

## Adaptation and Adjustment

The uncertainty of the initial symptoms and the brief sense of relief at having a name for them are often followed quickly by shock and disbelief. Deep down, we all think of ourselves as invulnerable to illness. It is difficult for a robust, healthy 30-year-old to accept the fact that he or she has a chronic illness that is progressive and potentially disabling. Most people with MS will assure you that they never really "accept" it (any more than they would accept a lifelong electrical storm that sends periodic lightning bolts into their home). What people eventually seem to do is to confront the reality of the disease and learn to adapt to its presence in their lives. This adaptation is important because without it the processes of coping and effective problem-solving can be short-circuited. . . .

MS sufferers must eventually confront the reality of the disease and learn to adapt to its presence in their lives. (© Celia Mannings/ Alamy)

## Self-Image Impacted

Multiple sclerosis is a tough pill to swallow, in part because it is so "personal." MS-related limitations can interfere with many cherished abilities, including walking, seeing, controlling the bladder, or driving a car. The person with MS may find many valued facets of his or her self-image undermined by these changes. "If I can't play outside with my kids (go on a class trip . . . coach a team . . . bake a cake), what kind of parent am I?" is the sort of question people may ask themselves. Sadness, frustration, anger, and feelings of worthlessness can ensue. Family members may find it hard to comprehend this intense inner struggle for the survival of a positive sense of self. They may see only its external signs, (e.g., irritability, emotional and social withdrawal), or a loss of interest in everyday activities.

Fortunately, for most people who have MS, disease-related changes *challenge* but do not *overwhelm* the self-image. Why? Because people are usually able to find other parts of themselves that they value, many of which are not physical. A mother with MS, for example, may learn that being a good parent does not just mean cooking elaborate meals or driving car pools, but is more directly related to providing the love and structure that children need to feel secure and realize their potential. A man who prided himself on his athletic abilities may discover a love of reading or a talent for writing that he never knew he had.

## Grief Phase

The process of renewing the self-image usually entails a period of grieving for those cherished abilities that have been compromised. Loss is a major issue for people living with MS. Many people feel that they have been robbed of their future. This loss of the future does not refer to premature death, which is rare in MS, but to the loss of their prior expectations for how life was likely to unfold. A person with MS might have had a promising career as a musician or a physician but now must follow a different path.

Grief is a healing and restorative process, but one that is accompanied by pain and sadness. Family members may experience some discomfort during this grieving process since it is often associated with a turning inward and feeling blue. However, grieving is critical to adjustment and may occur many times during the course of MS as the person is called upon to cope with new losses. . . .

## Temporary Stability

Dealing with emotions is an important part of the adjustment and coping process, but it is not the *only* part. In addition to coping with their emotions, people living with MS are generally called upon to make a variety of concrete changes in their day-to-day routines. When people are first impacted by MS symptoms, the disease may feel like a huge, looming monster that uses all the space in the family's life. There may be so much that needs to be done differently—such as getting from one place to another, managing tasks at home or at work, or enjoying leisure activities—that MS always seems to be in the way and underfoot. As people gradually make the necessary changes, however, and become accustomed to some modified ways of doing things, it becomes somewhat easier to "sweep MS into a corner." Although MS is never going to go away, the family can reach the point where the disease no longer drains quite as much attention and emotional energy. At that point, people are able to continue with their lives, secure in the fact that although MS is a *part* of their lives, it does not have to be the whole of it.

The ability to "sweep MS into a corner"—or "keep it in its place"—may last only as long as the disease is quiet and stable. With each significant change or loss, the disease looms large once again, requiring people to repeat the process of grieving and adaptation. Some have described life with MS as a kind of emotional roller coaster, defined by all the dips and turns of this unpredictable disease. . . .

## Emotional Changes

The distinction between emotional *responses* and emotional *changes* is somewhat arbitrary. In the previous section, we talked about some of the emotional responses that are most common in MS (i.e., those that almost everyone goes through at one time or another in the ongoing adjustment process). They are referred to as *responses* because it is assumed that they involve reactions to the altered life circumstances brought on by MS. In this section, some of the less common emotional experiences that can occur in MS are discussed. These include more serious emotional changes, along with a few that have a physiological basis rather than being reactions to the stress of the disease. In reality, there is a great deal of overlap among these various categories of emotional experiences. Moreover, we are often guessing when we attribute a specific cause to any emotion because we do not know for certain what is caused by stress and what is the result of demyelination. You may go through your entire life without experiencing any of the things described in this section. However, if these changes are part of your life with MS, the discussion that follows should help you understand what is happening and why.

## Varieties of Depression

The term depression is used in a variety of ways. In everyday language, the term is used loosely to refer to feeling down in the dumps. You might hear someone say, "Oh, she's depressed because she got a C on her final exam." This is not depression in the technical sense, but rather a situational and transient sadness or "dysphoria." In contrast, clinical depression (or major depressive disorder) is a serious and, at times, life-threatening psychiatric condition that meets specific diagnostic criteria. These criteria include profound sadness, loss of interest in everyday activities, changes in appetite and sleep patterns, feelings of worthlessness and/or guilt, lassitude, and thoughts of death or suicide. Major depressive disorder is more common in MS than in either the general population or among other disability groups. Research has shown that upward of half of all people with MS will have a full-blown, major depressive episode during the course of their illness. People are at particular risk for these episodes during exacerbations. The person who is in a major depressive episode may be unable to function and may withdraw from daily life and social interactions.

While such episodes are generally self-limited, there is considerable research showing that medication, either alone or in combination with psychotherapy, can help to shorten the episode and prevent or delay future episodes. In this situation, psychotherapy does not mean going to a support group, peer counselor, or other relatively informal form of intervention. Generally, a psychiatrist should be consulted and psychotherapy may be indicated with a mental health professional (e.g. psychiatrist, psychologist, or social worker). . . .

## Bipolar Disorder

Bipolar disorder is a relatively rare condition that is related to depression. It may be characterized by alternating periods of depression and mania, or just mania. Manic episodes are usually characterized by some combination of the following: unrealistic optimism; agitation and/or irritability; hyperactivity; sleeplessness; non-stop or rapid talking; a tendency to start myriad projects that are never completed; and uncontrolled expenditures of money. Bipolar disorder is more common in people who have MS than in the general population. It is generally treated using a mood-stabilizing drug such as lithium or divalproex sodium, although an antidepressant may also be necessary if there are depressive episodes. Manic episodes can be frightening and disruptive for everyone in the family, particularly when uncontrolled spending is part of the pattern. In this situation, legal safeguards should probably be considered to protect the financial stability of the family.

## Suicide

Suicide—contemplated, attempted, and completed—is thought to be more common in MS than in the general population. A study in Denmark found that completed suicide was twice as common among people with MS than in the general public. In recent years, additional interest in this subject has been generated by the controversy over assisted suicide. Thoughts about suicide are so frequent in MS because of the high rates of clinical depression and because of the ways in which MS can erode quality of life and cast a pall over the future.

It is beyond the scope of this chapter to enter into the philosophical debate concerning the "right" to commit suicide. We do know that suicidal feelings may pass when mood improves or one's life situation takes a turn for the better. Thus, the goal for all concerned—those with MS, their family members, and their healthcare providers—should be to ensure that the quality of life is the best that it can be, given any limitations imposed by the disease. Effective symptom management and emotional support are essential factors affecting quality of life. All those who live or work with MS need to be aware that active intervention and support are of particular importance at those times when suicide seems like the only viable route.

## Mood Swings

Family members have long complained that one of the most difficult things to deal with are the mood swings of the person with MS. While everyone in the world probably has mood swings from time to time, people with MS

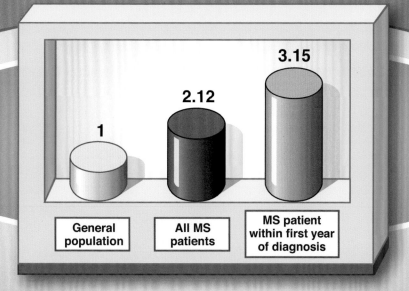

## Suicide Risk as Measured by Standardized Mortality Ratio

1 — General population

2.12 — All MS patients

3.15 — MS patient within first year of diagnosis

Taken from: H. Brønnum-Hansen et al., "Suicide Among Danes with Multiple Sclerosis," *Journal of Neurology, Neurosurgery, and Psychiatry*, 2005.

seem to be at greater risk for them. Is this the result of some complex alteration in brain structure, or just the frustration that goes along with disability? We do not know. Whatever the cause, the bursts of irritability, anger, sadness, and frustration can make family life very unpleasant. There is no easy solution to this problem. Family counseling and support groups are often helpful. A mood-stabilizing medication such as divalproex sodium or one of the SSRI [selective serotonin reuptake inhibitor] antidepressants is sometimes recommended. Most important are awareness and understanding on the part of all concerned, of the strong feelings that are being expressed. Quite often, exploration of these feelings will suggest possible ways to resolve some of them, thereby improving quality of life for the family as a whole.

# CHAPTER 2

# Controversies Concerning Multiple Sclerosis

# A Leaky Gut May Be the Cause of Multiple Sclerosis

## Ashton F. Embry

The cause of multiple sclerosis remains uncertain. Many alternative health practitioners think they can trace it back to what they term "leaky gut syndrome." In the following viewpoint Ashton F. Embry proposes that a leaky gut is the first key step on the path to multiple sclerosis. The problem, he says, is that tiny bits of allergy-provoking food slip through the lining of the intestine. Once in the body's circulatory system, they trigger the immune system to go into action, and when this happens repeatedly, he contends, the immune system begins to penetrate the blood-brain barrier, and multiple sclerosis results. According to Embry, the gut becomes leaky as a result of various assaults from allergenic foods, alcohol, drugs, and pathogens. He recommends a highly restricted diet, followed by ingestion of various nutritional supplements to cure the syndrome and bolster the immune system. Embry had been a geological research scientist for nearly three decades when his son was diagnosed with MS. He then turned his attention to researching the causes of the disease and became convinced that food allergens play a crucial role.

*Photo on facing page. A critical strategy to halt autoimmune reactions involves not eating foods such as dairy products, grains, yeast, and eggs, all of which can mimic the body's proteins. (© Photononstop/ SuperStock)*

**SOURCE:** Ashton F. Embry, "Multiple Sclerosis—Best Bet Treatment," *Direct-MS*, 2008. Reproduced by permission.

T he formulation of an effective treatment for MS [multiple sclerosis] clearly depends on knowing the cause of the disease. The treatment which is suggested in this essay assumes that dietary factors are the main cause of MS onset and progression because such a cause best fits the extensive epidemiological data base and is theoretically plausible.

The basic elements of a dietary model for MS are the escape of intact food proteins through a leaky gut and subsequent activation of the immune system. The immune system is activated against tissue in the central nervous system due to molecular similarities between the food proteins and self-proteins in the CNS [central nervous system]. Access to the CNS through the blood-brain barrier (BBB) may be aided by . . . hypersensitivity reactions also precipitated by foods.

The keys to combating MS are thus halting the activation of the immune system and healing and strengthening various systems including the gut, the BBB and the immune system. . . .

## Leaky Gut Hazard

A leaky gut refers to increased permeability of the intestinal tract and such a condition allows food protein fragments to pass between intestinal cells into the circulatory system. Laboratories offer intestinal permeability tests, although it may be easier to assume you have a leaky gut and to take steps to heal it.

Increased intestinal permeability has various causes such as ingestion of allergenic foods, candida overgrowth, alcohol consumption, infection, parasites, trauma and usage of non-steroidal anti-inflammatory drugs such as Aspirin. Notably, lectins (a type of protein) found in grains and legumes also increase gut permeability. It is critical to eliminate the source of the problem (e.g. candida [yeast] overgrowth). In some cases this is straight forward but for food allergies it can be more difficult. . . .

## Healing Supplements

Once the source of the gut irritation has been removed (e.g. food allergens) then it is important to take supplements which help to heal the gut. . . . Some of these include acidophilus, glutamine, glutathione, grape seed extract, evening primrose oil, fish oil, fiber and enzymes.

The second and perhaps most important strategy for halting autoimmune reactions is to stop eating foods which potentially contain proteins which can mimic self- proteins. Unfortunately there is no test which can be administered to establish which foods may be problematic for a given individual. Thus it is essential to eliminate all foods which have the potential to mimic self. These foods include all dairy products, all grains, all legumes (e.g. beans), eggs and yeast. For grains the most problematic ones are glutenous ones which

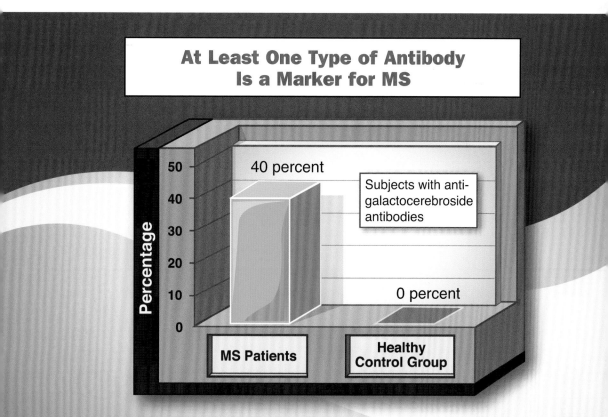

Taken from: Til Menge et al., "Antibody Responses Against Galactocerebroside Are Potential Stage-Specific Biomarkers in Multiple Sclerosis," *Journal of Allergy and Clinical Immunology*, August 2005.

include wheat, rye, barley and oats. These must be avoided without fail. Rice seems like the safest of the non-gluten grains but even it can be problematic for some. . . .

## Limiting Fat Intake

In general saturated fats and trans-fatty acids (altered unsaturated fatty acids) seem to promote inflammatory reactions whereas polyunsaturated fats modulate such reactions. Thus it is important to keep the daily intake of saturated fat to less than 15 grams a day. This essentially necessitates the avoidance of all red meat and dark meat from chicken and turkey. Monosaturated oils (extra virgin olive oil) and polyunsaturated oils (unrefined sunflower and safflower oil) can be used with a maximum consumption of about 60 g [grams] a day. All margarines should be avoided. Omega three essential fatty acids tend to be deficient in many and these are mainly derived from fish and flax oil. Notably, fish oil has been found to be very beneficial in controlling another autoimmune disease, Crohn's disease.

> **FAST FACT**
>
> "Leaky gut syndrome" is not a legitimate medical diagnosis in the view of most doctors, but neither has its existence been ruled out by medical science.

## Bolstering the System

Experiments with animals have shown that there are three related chemicals, anthocyanosides, proanthocyanidins and procyanidolic oligomers, which strengthen the BBB. These chemical are found in blueberries, cherries, blackberries, grapes and the bark and needles of certain pine trees. They are currently available as encapsulated supplements called bilberry, grape seed extract and pycnogenol. These supplements and/or substantial quantities of the above fruits should be ingested daily to help strengthen the BBB.

The anthocyanosides and proanthocyanidins act as very powerful anti-oxidants, block enzyme actions, and bind with the BBB, and it is these properties which likely result in their beneficial effect on the BBB. Other supplements which are anti-oxidants (much less powerful) include vitamin A (cod liver oil), vitamin C (with bioflavonoids) and vitamin E. These, along with vitamin B complex and vitamin D, should be taken daily.

Because MS is basically caused by a malfunctioning immune system, it is worthwhile to strengthen the immune system such that it operates in a more normal fashion Most important in this regard is the healthy functioning of the suppression side of the system which is programmed to shut down harmful autoimmune reactions as soon as possible.

Minerals such as zinc and selenium, help strengthen the immune system, and also may well have value in

Some claim that fruits like blueberries produce chemicals that strengthen the blood-brain barrier (BBB) and should be eaten daily to help fight the symptoms of MS. (Image copyright Olga Lyubkina, 2009. Used under license from Shutterstock.com.)

warding off viral infections. It has also been suggested that herbs such as goldenseal and echinacea have value in strengthening the immune system. One problem with these herbs is that they may cause hypersensitivities (goldenseal is closely related to ragweed) and questions still remain concerning the wisdom in taking these herbs over a long time period. I would suggest caution in their use for MS treatment with echinacea perhaps being the safest herb to use to strengthen the immune system.

# Trauma May Be a Key Cause of Multiple Sclerosis

## S.J.M. Weatherby and C.P. Hawkins

Unlikely as it might seem, trauma may be a cause of multiple sclerosis. In the following viewpoint medical professors S.J.M. Weatherby and C.P. Hawkins lay out the chain of events in which a blow to the head can lead to multiple sclerosis. First, they note, a person must be unfortunate enough to lose control of killer T cells in his or her immune system. This precondition is not enough to cause MS, because ordinarily such cells cannot get past the membrane that protects the brain. Trauma, however, may breach the so-called blood-brain barrier, allowing T cells to get in and wreak havoc on the central nervous system. The hypothesis has yet to be confirmed by evidence, which has so far shown only minor connections between trauma and MS, but the researchers say more rigorous work on the question is needed. Weatherby is a medical researcher at the University Department of Clinical Neurology in the Queen Elizabeth Hospital of Birmingham, England. Hawkins is professor of clinical neurology at the Research Institute for Science and Technology in Medicine, Keele University, England.

**SOURCE:** S.J.M Weatherby and C.P. Hawkins, "Does Trauma Trigger Multiple Sclerosis? 1: A Controversy," *British Journal of Hospital Medicine,* vol. 64, October 10, 2003, pp. 581–84. Reproduced by permission.

A confocal light micrograph of a section of the forebrain shows a breakdown in the blood-brain barrier. The lighter areas indicate leakage from the blood vessels into the surrounding brain tissue. (C.J. Guerin, PhD, MRC Toxicology Unit/ Photo Researchers, Inc.)

Multiple sclerosis (MS) is the commonest neurological disorder affecting young adults, and all hospital physicians and GPs [general practitioners] are likely to have experience of caring for these patients.

The question of whether trauma triggers onset or exacerbations in MS is frequently asked by MS patients of their medical advisors. It is important both from the scientific standpoint and also in terms of counselling patients. It remains a controversial issue and has been the subject of a number of medicolegal cases. . . .

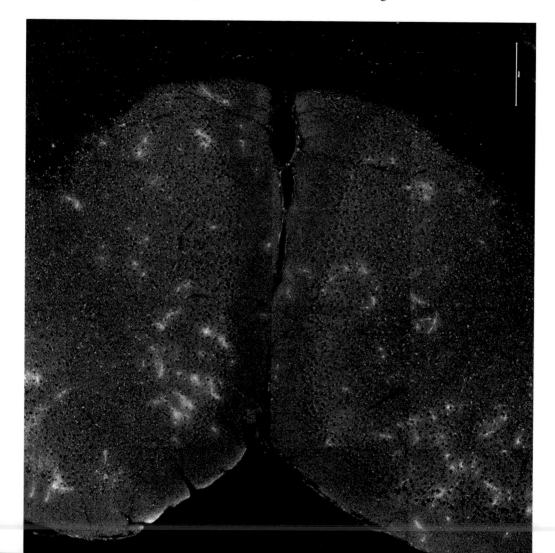

It is a natural tendency to blame any illness on antecedent events. In a condition of uncertain aetiology [cause] this is particularly tempting and the underlying causes of MS currently remain unclear. Patients may be genetically susceptible, as a number of genome screens attest. However, even the highest estimates put the genetic contribution at no more than 40%. The environment therefore plays a significant role. . . .

It is believed that one of the first events to occur in the pathology of MS is dysregulation of the immune system, which allows T cells specific for myelin basic protein to be activated in the periphery.

> ## FAST FACT
>
> Whether or not trauma causes MS, strong evidence shows that MS patients suffer more trauma than the average person. One study found that MS patients experience two to three times as many incidents of physical trauma as the control group.

## Trauma to the Brain

Although the healthy blood-brain barrier is impermeable to large molecules there is evidence that activated T cells [from the immune system] are able to cross the blood-brain barrier and enter the CNS [central nervous system]. Within the CNS they attack the myelin basic protein and so cause damage and demyelination.

If trauma causes a breakdown in the blood-brain barrier, patients constitutionally susceptible to MS ('potential demyelinators') may be vulnerable to trauma either triggering disease onset or exacerbations.

## What Is the Evidence?

Broadly speaking the evidence can be divided into that from animal experiments, observations in humans and magnetic resonance imaging (MRI) studies. Evidence suggesting blood-brain barrier breakdown has been found in animals suffering mechanical brain injury too slight to produce other neuropathological changes. This has been taken to suggest that physical trauma may cause new lesions that would not have otherwise occurred but for trauma. The finding that spontaneous concussive CNS injury causes diffuse microscopic lesions of blood vessels that would escape notice on superficial examination of the brain may suggest that minor trauma can be relevant. Significant increases in blood-brain barrier permeability in animal brains subject to whiplash injury have been reported and may be clinically important because whiplash injury is a frequent occurrence in road traffic accidents. . . .

## Whiplash at Fault?

A cohort of 39 [human] cases have been described in which MS onset or MS exacerbations bore a temporal relationship to hyperextension-hyperflexion neck injury [typical in whiplash]. Close anatomical correspondence between MS plaques and compression of the spinal cord by spondylosis, discs or whiplash injuries to the neck have been noted [in MRI studies].

## Question of Timing

Invoking the blood-brain barrier mechanism, the potential 'window of opportunity' for physical trauma to provoke MS symptoms would be the time period that the blood-brain barrier was permeable to autoreactive [rogue] T cells. Signal enhancement (following gadolinium contrast) is an indicator of blood-brain barrier breakdown. The duration of enhancement of a new lesion generally lasts from 2 weeks to 3 months, but for most lesions it is between 2 and 6 weeks. It would therefore appear that if an exacerbation were to be caused by physical trauma it would be likely to occur within 3 months. . . .

## Evidence from Studies

An 8-year study was performed to prospectively record all episodes of physical trauma and to measure the effect on exacerbation rate and progression of MS. One hundred and seventy MS patients and a group of matched controls were followed. The number of exacerbations in the 3- and 6-month periods after an episode of trauma (termed an 'at risk' period; AR) were compared with the number of exacerbations at other times (when 'not at risk'; NAR).

The incidence of trauma was found to be approximately three times higher in MS patients than controls. No significant relationship was found between trauma and MS deterioration in the AR period. In a subgroup with more frequent exacerbations a higher proportion of relapses were observed in the NAR period, and a statistically significant negative correlation between traumatic episodes and exacerbations was reported. When a subanalysis of trauma type was performed electric shocks were significantly associated with exacerbation during a 3-month but not 6-month AR period, and no other trauma types were found to have significant associations. . . .

## Connection Disputed

A subcommittee of the American Academy of Neurology reviewed the evidence linking trauma and MS. Only class II evidence was considered (case-control or cohort studies), there being no class I evidence. Essentially the conclusions were 'that there was strong evidence limiting any posited association between serious head trauma and onset of MS to no more than 1.3%' and that the 'association between serious head trauma and MS exacerbation is similarly limited to no more than a fraction of a percent of cases'.

It is often said that negative studies cannot exclude an association between variables. Furthermore it must be pointed out that the epidemiological studies have been criticized for being underpowered, for examining 'inappropriate or irrelevant trauma' (e.g. lumbar disc surgery) and including trauma that is 'too mild' (e.g. abrasions and lacerations). As the American Academy of Neurology

## The Probability of an MS Flare-Up Rises After Stress

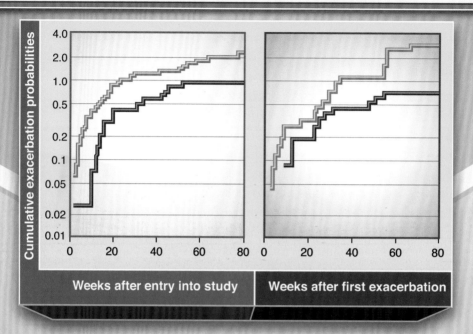

Taken from: D. Buljevac et al., "Self-Reported Stressful Life Events and Exacerbations in Multiple Sclerosis," *British Medical Journal*, September 20, 2003.

review was based to a large extent on the epidemiological studies described above, it has been subject to similar criticisms. . . .

## Case Remains Open

In spite of data from epidemiological studies and a report from the American Academy of Neurology, the question of whether a patient's MS would have developed or was aggravated by trauma remains the subject of sometimes intense consideration. The level of evidence required by courts may differ from that needed from a scientific standpoint. Arguably medicolegal issues could be of more immediate relevance to a patient, and may be a major driving force behind the vigour of the debate.

# Infection May Be a Key Cause of Multiple Sclerosis

**Jock Murray**

Among the possible causes of multiple sclerosis, infection has long been a chief suspect. In the following viewpoint physician Jock Murray discusses the long search for a culprit. Research going back as far as 1863, Murray notes, has proposed various answers to the puzzle. The search for an infectious cause alone has turned up dozens of possibilities. However, no one has been able to pin down any one pathogen as the cause. In fact, Murray says, despite the statistical evidence of population studies, research on particular viruses has produced weak results. Nevertheless, he argues that infection is likely to be the cause of some if not all cases of MS. Murray is professor of medicine at Dalhousie University in Canada.

It is difficult to think of an aetiological [causal] theory that has not been suggested to explain multiple sclerosis. Disconcertingly, however, many of the aetiological

**SOURCE:** Jock Murray, "Infection as a Cause of Multiple Sclerosis," *British Medical Journal,* vol. 325, November 16, 2002, p. 1,128. Copyright © 2002 British Medical Association. Reproduced by permission.

questions asked over 150 years ago are still unanswered. Is the disease due to a vascular defect as initially suggested by [pathologist Eduard] Rindfleisch in 1863, who noted a blood vessel in the centre of each plaque, or is it a defect in the glial tissue as argued by [neurologist Jean-Martin] Charcot in 1868 after he viewed and drew the glial and nerve changes under his microscope? [Researcher Herman] Oppenheim was certain that multiple sclerosis was caused by environmental toxins. In the middle of the 20th century interest centred around the possibility that it was

The controversy over what causes MS has been around since the 1860s. Dr. Jean-Martin Charcot theorized that a defect in the glial tissue was a cause of MS. (Imagno/Getty Images)

an immunological disease and, more recently, a genetic disease.

Perhaps the most enduring questions concern a potential infectious agent. In 1894 Pierre Marie, a former student of Charcot, argued strongly that infection was the cause of multiple sclerosis and that those who disagreed had not read his papers. He did not know the specific infective agent but was certain that a treatment would soon be available in the form of a "vaccine of Pasteur or lymph of Koch." William Gowers and other writers believed that an infection could aggravate multiple sclerosis but was not the cause. There was a flurry of reports of virus and spirochete isolations and transmissions in the early decades of the 20th century, but none stood the tests of time and reproducibility. Absence of evidence is not evidence of absence, however, and the infection theory remained strong because it seemed to best fit the developing scenario. Every new antibiotic and antiviral agent is given a trial in multiple sclerosis. Viral infections have been suspected in clusters of cases, including the "epidemic"-like appearance and disappearance of a cluster of cases on the Faroe Islands.

## FAST FACT

Some researchers believe they have evidence that multiple sclerosis is a sexually transmitted disease.

## Many Suspects

Intriguing epidemiological [population studies] but weak virological and immunological evidence has resulted in a bewildering list of usual suspects including measles, rabies, scrapie-like agent, Carp agent, paramyxovirus, coronavirus, Epstein-Barr virus, herpes zoster, herpes simplex virus, human herpesvirus 6, rubella, mumps, canine distemper, Marek's Semliki forest virus, animal and human retroviruses, and human T cell lymphoma virus type 1. Although multiple sclerosis was on the top of the list of "most likely" when the concept of slow virus infection was being formulated in the 1960s, the transmission experiments were all negative. Interestingly, Stanley Pruziner, recent Nobel laureate for his work on prions [infectious agents composed of protein], does not have multiple sclerosis on his personal list of possible prion diseases.

Current scientific interest is focused on chlamydia pneumonia and the Epstein-Barr virus. Epstein-Barr virus has been under suspicion for over two decades, and recently it was noted that patients with multiple sclerosis had an increase in respiratory infections before the onset of multiple sclerosis and a fivefold increase over controls in infectious mononucleosis. Is this an indication of a specific role for Epstein-Barr virus or just an indication of a non-specific response of the immune system in patients with multiple sclerosis?

A vascular theory for multiple sclerosis resurfaced with the development of anticoagulants, replaced in the 1960s by an interest in dietary therapies, which had a vascular defect as part of the rationale. Recent work is again focused on the vascular changes as a basis of the breakdown of the blood-brain barrier that precedes the inflammation and demyelination in a multiple sclerosis plaque. Proponents of the infection theory would add that an infection could be the initial event that precipitates this process.

## Multiple Factors at Work

Over the past century and a half, bolstered by a body of observations and anecdotes, proponents of aetiological theories have focused on environmental toxins, "neuropathic constitution," physical and emotional stresses, circulating myelinotoxins and lipolytic enzymes, dietary factors, and vascular thrombosis. Early writers all noted occasional cases in a family but dismissed these as coincidental. Recent research is convincing in showing the risk in siblings and fraternal twins to be about 2–5%, much higher than in the normal population, but about 30% in identical twins, a clear

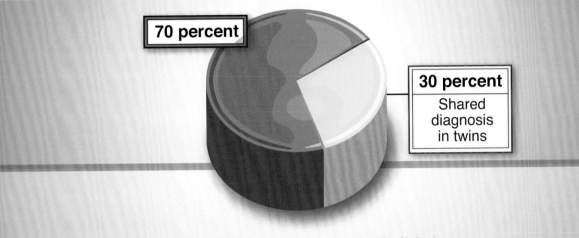

## Fewer than One-third of Identical Twins Both Get MS

70 percent

30 percent
Shared diagnosis in twins

Taken from: Nikolaos Grigoriadis and Georgios M. Hadjigeorgiou, "Virus-Mediated Autoimmunity in Multiple Sclerosis," *Journal of Autoimmune Diseases*, February 19, 2006.

indication of a genetic factor. But why don't the two thirds of genetically predisposed identical twins get the disease? The conclusion is that multiple sclerosis is a complex trait, determined by multiple genes and an environmental factor. Is the other factor an infection?

There has been a reluctance to dispense with any theory when the answer is still unknown. So a current popular overarching theory postulates a genetically predisposed individual who develops a viral infection that disrupts the vascular relations in the blood-brain barrier and initiates an immune reaction that continues as a waxing and waning destructive process that damages myelin, and perhaps more importantly in the long term, the axons. But just as a workable and testable theory has evolved, important work by an international group implies potentially four pathological patterns of multiple sclerosis. So we must add to the quandary the possibility that we may be dealing with different disorders with different causes. No one ever said medicine was simple.

# Faulty Genes May Be at the Root of Multiple Sclerosis

**Sabin Russell**

Scientists have long suspected that a genetic predisposition plays a role in the development of multiple sclerosis. In the following viewpoint Sabin Russell describes a breakthrough piece of research that confirms the part that one gene plays in raising the risk that a person will develop the disease and points to two other genes as suspects. The research involved scanning the genomes of more than twelve thousand people, some with MS and others not, to discover associations between the presence of the disease and certain genetic variants. The link between the suspect genes and MS was not strong, Russell notes—many healthy people also have the variants —but it was clear enough for scientists to conclude that genes, while not an exclusive cause, do lie at the root of the disease. Russell is a staff medical writer for *The San Francisco Chronicle*.

New DNA scanning technologies, which have uncovered genetic traits tied to a growing list of human ailments, have spotted three gene mutations that may raise the risk of a person developing

**SOURCE:** Sabin Russell, "3 Genes Linked to Multiple Sclerosis," *San Francisco Chronicle*, July 30, 2007. Reproduced by permission.

multiple sclerosis, the most common neurological disease among young and middle-age adults.

The discoveries strengthen the widely held but unproven theory that MS is an autoimmune disease in which infection-fighting blood cells mistakenly attack the protein sheaths that protect our nerves.

## Confirmation of Genetic Role

In three papers released online Sunday [July 29, 2007], international teams of researchers report how new experiments have reconfirmed the role of one gene in raising the risk of MS, and stirred suspicions about two other immune system genes that may contribute to the disease.

"I think these studies, together, really change the landscape of multiple sclerosis research," said Dr. Stephen Hauser, chairman of the UCSF [University of California–San Francisco] Department of Neurology. He was lead author of the study released Sunday by the *New England Journal of Medicine*, and also a contributor to one of two studies also published online by the British medical journal *Nature Genetics*.

Multiple sclerosis strikes women twice as often as men and afflicts about 400,000 Americans and 2.5 million people worldwide. Sufferers are plagued by chronic and progressive symptoms, ranging from muscle weakness and fatigue to complete loss of mobility.

## More than 12,000 Subjects

Hauser's study involved an international consortium of MS researchers, who scanned the full complement of genes in each of 12,360 subjects, a group that included patients with multiple sclerosis and their parents as well as unrelated healthy volunteers. The gene-scanning machines— made by Affymetrix Inc. of Santa Clara [California]— are capable of picking out in each person any of 500,000 common genetic mutations that researchers have identified in the human population.

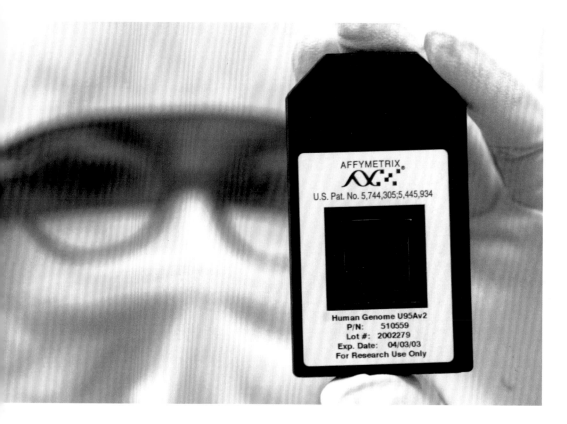

AFFYMETRIX
U.S. Pat. No. 5,744,305;5,445,934

Human Genome U95Av2
P/N:    510559
Lot #:  2002279
Exp. Date:  04/03/03
For Research Use Only

The new gene-scanning technologies developed by Affymetrix Inc. allow DNA fragments to be infused into pieces of glass for genetic research. (AP Images)

These mutations serve as beacons on the vast genetic landscape, signaling that somewhere nearby on the genome there is a specific DNA sequence that is different from the one carried by the majority of the human population. When these beacons show up in large numbers of people suffering from a disease such as multiple sclerosis, it is evidence that a mutated gene close to the marker may be contributing to the illness.

The gene-scans carried out by Hauser and his colleagues flagged three genes that appeared more often in MS patients than in the general population. The strongest association was found for a genetic region called HLA-DR. One particular genetic mutation there appears to raise the risk of multiple sclerosis nearly sixfold.

In 1972, scientists using much more primitive gene-hunting techniques had already isolated this region on the human chromosome. The most recent study reaffirms the accuracy of those earlier studies.

## Additional Suspect Genes

But the new reports are the first to prove there was small, but significant, association between two other previously suspect genes and susceptibility to MS. One gene causes

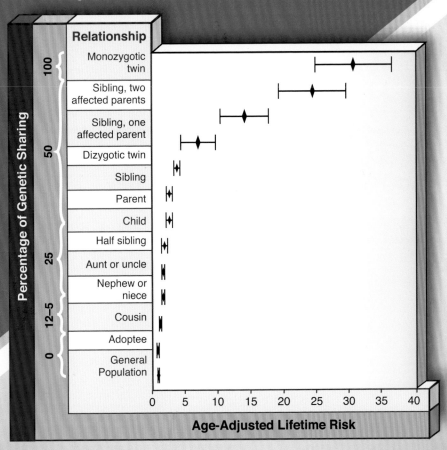

**Genetic Sharing and MS Risk**

The closer the genetic link to someone with MS, the higher an individual's risk of developing the disease.

Taken from: Multiple Sclerosis Information Trust, "Research in Multiple Sclerosis," January 21, 2008.

white blood cells to attract an immune system–stimulating chemical called IL-2, while the other attracts the protein IL-7. Both genes are switches that regulate the immune system.

Although an individual's odds of contracting multiple sclerosis are low, the studies suggest that those who carry the variant genes of IL-2 or IL-7 nudge their risk upward about 20 percent.

Hauser was especially intrigued by the IL-7 connection because he participated in a second study, published simultaneously in *Nature Genetics*, that zeroed in on the same gene using a different laboratory technique. In a third study released Sunday, also in *Nature Genetics*, Scandinavian researchers also confirmed a link to the IL-7 gene.

The signals that found an association between MS and these two immune system switches were just a whisper compared to the powerful connection between the disease and the HLA gene, which also regulates the body's system of inflammatory defense against invading microbes. . . .

## Weak but Important Link

Hauser said that while the association between these immune switch genes and multiple sclerosis is small, it is still important. "Many genes, all with small effects, may be working together to make an individual susceptible," he said. "I think everything that we find is important, even if it is subtle."

Dr. John Richert, executive vice president of the National MS Society in New York, said the results were good news, even if the association of gene to disease seems weak. "These numbers mean we have a long way to go to understand full genetic susceptibility, but we've learned how to go forward," he said.

Similar gene-scans, known as genome-wide association studies, recently have picked out genetic variations linked to coronary artery disease, prostate cancer, obesity and natural resistance to HIV, the virus that causes AIDS.

"The breakneck pace of discovery will be continuing . . . with anticipated findings for many cancers, cardiovascular diseases, and neurological diseases," wrote Dr. Eric Topol, a cardiac surgeon who heads the Scripps Genomic Medicine Institute in La Jolla (San Diego County) in a July 11 [2007] commentary in the *Journal of the American Medical Association.* "In aggregate, these studies have the potential to radically change medicine."

# Hyperbaric Oxygen Treatments Are Effective in Treating Multiple Sclerosis

## William S. Maxfield

The use of oxygen at high pressure to treat the symptoms of multiple sclerosis is rejected by most authorities. In the following viewpoint, however, a physician advocates the use of so-called hyperbaric oxygen therapy. William S. Maxfield explains that he became acquainted with the technique while in the navy and later tried it to help his ailing father-in-law. The apparent success of the treatment led him to create a facility to offer the therapy to the public in south Florida. Over a couple of decades, Maxfield says, hyperbaric oxygen therapy has proved effective for the great majority of his multiple sclerosis patients. While not a cure, it does relieve symptoms, he states, and prolongs the time that sufferers are able to be fully mobile and in control of their bodily functions. Maxfield is a physician and certified radiologist.

The use of hyperbaric oxygen therapy (HBOT) for treatment of multiple sclerosis was advocated by Richard A. Neubauer, M.D., in the late 1970s. I be-

**SOURCE:** William S. Maxfield, "Hyperbaric Oxygen Therapy for Multiple Sclerosis: My Experience," *Journal of American Physicians and Surgeons*, vol. 10, Winter 2005, p. 116. Reproduced by permission.

came acquainted with Dr. Neubauer when searching for a solution for my father-in-law's problem of loss of balance and deteriorating speech. After evaluation at four of the top neurological centers in the Southeast gave no definite diagnosis and no offer of treatment, I looked for a center performing hyperbaric oxygen therapy (HBOT).

I first learned about HBOT while on active duty in the Navy, when I was part of the plutonium decontamination team. Later, when I was chief of radiation therapy at Ochsner Clinic and Foundation Hospital in New Orleans, HBOT was planned as an adjunct to radiation therapy in the new department.

A mother and daughter prepare to undergo hyperbaric oxygen treatment in a chamber at a medical center in Hawaii. The viewpoint author created such a facility to treat MS patients in Florida. (Marco Garcia/MCT/Landov)

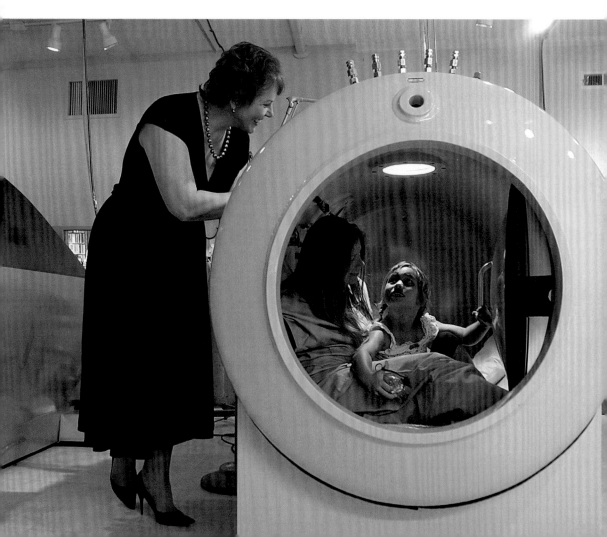

My father-in-law's symptoms were well controlled for three years after a course of HBOT at Dr. Neubauer's center. At that time, it was customary to wait until symptoms recurred before providing additional treatment. Since then, experience with multiple sclerosis (MS) patients has shown that periodic HBOT can provide better long-term results. My father-in-law's good years might have been extended had he received maintenance therapy.

## Symptomatic Relief

When I established Gulf South Radiation Therapy Center in Largo, Florida, in the early 1980s, our facility provided not only the first linear accelerator in Pinellas County, but also the first HBOT facility in the area. I was aware of Dr. Neubauer's report of excellent response in MS patients, but because I was not sure that HBOT was of benefit in that condition, I treated a number of MS patients without charge. I was pleased by the results. Although HBOT does not cure MS, my impression was that it provided significant symptomatic relief and delayed or decreased progression. I viewed it as being similar to the use of insulin or other antidiabetic medications in that regard.

Because of my interest in treating MS with HBOT, I joined the Gulf Coast Chapter of the MS Society, and after several years of membership was elected chapter chairman in 1985. This elevation in rank brought me to the attention of the National Multiple Sclerosis Society [NMSS]. When it learned that I practiced hyperbaric medicine and advocated HBOT for MS patients, the NMSS asked that I not be reelected upon completion of my term in 1986.

## Marked Improvement

Over the years, my experience with HBOT for MS has continued to be excellent. I estimate the response rate to be better than 80 percent, particularly with regard to regaining bladder control and increasing mobility and strength. The majority of neurologists that I dealt with, however, did not agree with my assessment. For example, one of my MS patients could barely walk from the parking lot into the building—about 60 feet—before HBOT was started. After 2 months of treatment, she was walking 2 miles on the beach. Nonetheless, her neurologist reported "no improvement" because she still had a wide-based gait and some minor neurological symptoms. With continued HBOT, her MS remained stable.

**FAST FACT**

A patient breathing pure oxygen at three times normal pressure in a hyperbaric oxygen chamber experiences fifteen times more oxygen in the blood than usual.

I now have 20 years of follow-up on two of my first MS patients. One continues to have minimal symptoms. Another, whose condition was more advanced, had been told that she would be bedridden in 6 months if she did not take methotrexate, a treatment that is no longer recommended. She opted for HBOT and other "alternative" treatments, completed her Ph.D., had two children, and continues to practice as a speech therapist, although she now uses a wheelchair. Her initial prognosis for remaining time until incapacitation was off by a factor of about 40.

## No Serious Complications

In my years of active practice using HBOT, both with my own patients and as a consultant for other centers, I am unaware of any significant complications from the use of HBOT for the MS patient. There is the well-recognized occurrence of an occasional seizure, one per 10,000 compressions. These seizures do not produce long-term sequelae [results], and indicate the need for lowering the treatment pressure.

Many of my patients switched to [the drug] Betaseron when it became available, but a significant number of these returned to HBOT when their symptoms progressed.

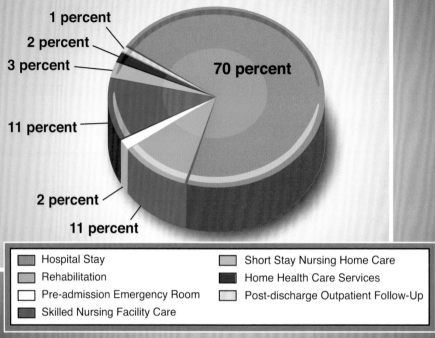

## Hospital Stays Are the Costliest Component of Treating MS

1 percent
2 percent
3 percent
70 percent
11 percent
2 percent
11 percent

| | | | |
|---|---|---|---|
| ▦ Hospital Stay | | ▦ Short Stay Nursing Home Care | |
| ▦ Rehabilitation | | ▦ Home Health Care Services | |
| ▢ Pre-admission Emergency Room | | ▦ Post-discharge Outpatient Follow-Up | |
| ▦ Skilled Nursing Facility Care | | | |

Taken from: Judith A. O'Brien et al., "Cost of Managing an Episode of Relapse in Multiple Sclerosis in the United States," *BMC Health Services Research*, September 2, 2003.

The NMSS still states that HBOT is ineffective in MS. I have learned, however, that some physicians who initially had an unfavorable view of HBOT in MS now serve as consultants to hyperbaric facilities.

## No Insurance Coverage

Insurance reimbursement for the use of HBOT in neurologic conditions has generally been unavailable. Precedents are being set, however. Blue Cross/Blue Shield of Texas bought a monoplace chamber for one of my MS patients. With HBOT, she was able to resume the active practice of law and has had minimal progression of her MS. One of my MS patients, who had a complete reversal of her MS symptoms with HBOT, sued Blue Cross/Blue Shield in Hillsborough County, Florida, for coverage of her HBOT costs. She was awarded full reimbursement plus payment for any additional HBOT that was needed.

The cost-effectiveness of HBOT may be improved by the development of the portable low-pressure chamber. Patients whose symptoms can be controlled at pressures of 1.25 to 1.3 atmospheres absolute (ATA) can, for a moderate investment, use a chamber at home. Chambers that provide higher pressures may soon be available.

In calculating cost-effectiveness, one must certainly consider the reports of patients who lived active, productive lives for years or decades rather than rapidly progressing to the point of needing nursing home care as their clinicians had predicted.

# Hyperbaric Oxygen Treatments Are Unproven for Treating Multiple Sclerosis

## Health Canada

The use of hyperbaric oxygen chambers is highly regulated under Canada's national health care system. In the following viewpoint the agency Health Canada explains why it approves hyperbaric treatment for only a handful of conditions and specifically excludes multiple sclerosis from the list. No scientific evidence supports the claim that hyperbaric oxygen therapy benefits those who suffer from multiple sclerosis, the agency says. Moreover, the treatments are costly and carry certain risks, so it recommends against them for MS patients. Health Canada is the agency in the Canadian federal government that administers that country's national health system.

While hyperbaric oxygen therapy is recognized as an effective treatment for 13 specific conditions listed below, the operators of some private clinics claim it can also be used to treat such con-

SOURCE: Health Canada/Santé Canada, "Hyperbaric Oxygen Therapy," *It's Your Health,* December 15, 2006. Reproduced with the permission of the Minister of Public Works and Government Services Canada, 2009.

ditions as multiple sclerosis, cerebral palsy, cancer, AIDS, stroke and migraine headaches. There is no scientific proof to support these claims.

Hyperbaric oxygen therapy is a well established medical treatment. In April 2005, the Undersea and Hyperbaric Medical Society recognized the therapy as an effective treatment for 13 specific conditions:

- embolisms (air or gas bubbles in the bloodstream, which may travel to the brain or lungs)
- carbon monoxide poisoning (from inhaling smoke or car exhaust)
- gas gangrene
- crush injury, Compartment Syndrome and other acute traumatic problems where blood flow is reduced or cut off (e.g., frostbite)
- decompression sickness (the bends)
- enhancement of healing for wounds such as diabetic foot ulcers
- exceptional blood loss (anemia)
- intracranial abscess (an accumulation of pus in the brain)
- necrotizing soft tissue infections (flesh-eating disease)
- osteomyelitis (bone infection)
- delayed radiation injury (e.g., radiation burns that develop after cancer therapy)
- skin grafts and flaps that are not healing well
- thermal burns (e.g., from fire or electrical sources)

## Pure Oxygen

The therapy promotes healing in these 13 conditions by delivering a high concentration of oxygen quickly and deeply into the affected areas of the body.

During treatment, a patient goes into a closed chamber. The atmospheric pressure inside the chamber is increased. When the pressure reaches the level prescribed for the treatment, the patient is given 100 percent oxygen to breathe for a set amount of time. The patient breathes the oxygen through a hood and is advised when to take "breaks" and breathe the regular air inside the chamber. Regular air is 21 percent oxygen.

Some hyperbaric chambers hold only one patient. Others can accommodate two or more people. On occasion, a care-giver will go into the chamber with a patient.

The duration of each treatment, the number of treatments and the pressure used all vary, depending on the patient's condition. Hyperbaric oxygen therapy treatments normally take place in hospitals or private clinics. . . .

## No Scientific Proof

Health Canada has reviewed the scientific evidence related to hyperbaric chambers. The evidence shows that chambers are effective in treating the 13 conditions recognized by the Undersea and Hyperbaric Medical Society. Therefore, Health Canada has issued medical device licences for hyperbaric chambers to treat only these 13 conditions. No device licences have been issued for the use of hyperbaric chambers to treat other conditions.

Be skeptical of anyone who advertises or offers hyperbaric oxygen therapy to treat conditions such as multiple sclerosis, cerebral palsy, cancer, AIDS, stroke or migraine headaches. At present there is no scientific proof that this therapy is useful in treating these other conditions.

It is very expensive to have treatments at a private clinic. People who pursue hyperbaric oxygen therapy for these other conditions may spend a lot of money for little

> **FAST FACT**
>
> After reviewing nine studies of the efficacy of hyperbaric oxygen therapy for multiple sclerosis, researchers concluded that there was no consistent evidence to confirm a beneficial effect.

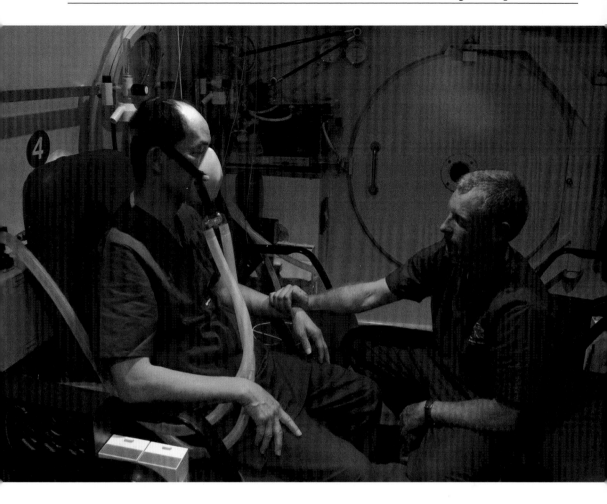

or no benefit. Even worse, they may delay, or in some cases not receive, proven treatments that could help them or their loved ones.

## Risky Treatment

When used to treat recognized medical conditions, hyperbaric oxygen therapy is generally safe, as long as:

- the chamber is properly installed according to municipal and provincial regulations;
- operators and attendants are properly trained; and,
- a certified hyperbaric physician is either on site, or can be reached easily and quickly.

Although there is evidence that hyperbaric oxygen therapy is useful in treating some medical conditions, experts in Canada's national health care system say no proof exists that it is effective in treating MS. (© **Louise Murray**/Alamy)

# Hyperbaric Oxygen Therapy (HBOT) Centers in the United States

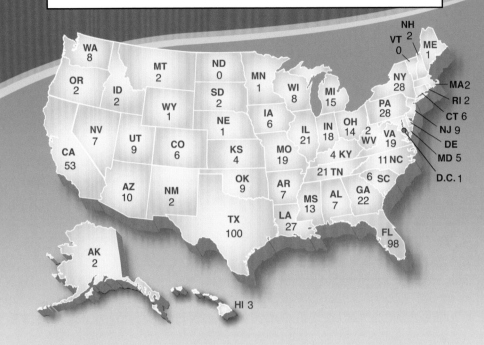

Taken from: Shien Guo, Michael A. Counte, Homer Schmitz, and Horng-Shiuann Wu, "Physician Adoption of Hyperbaric Oxygen Therapy in the Treatment of Chronic Wound," *Ostomy/Wound Management*, October 2005.

However, there are risks. Before consenting to treatment, you should consider these factors:

- Pressure inside the chamber can damage the middle and inner ear, nasal sinuses, lungs and teeth in both adults and children.

- Some people experience claustrophobia inside the chamber.

- The therapy may affect your eyes, for example by promoting nearsightedness or cataract growth.

- Because hyperbaric oxygen therapy affects blood sugar levels, diabetics should have their levels checked before and after treatment.

- A high concentration of oxygen can cause serious complications in some children who have congenital heart disease.

- Too much oxygen can sometimes, although rarely, lead to overload that can cause seizures and lung problems. This is usually prevented by having the patient take breaks to breathe normal air instead of pure oxygen.

- High concentrations of oxygen at elevated pressures can pose a risk of fire.

There is also a risk the chamber might explode if it has not been properly installed or if the staff is not properly trained. . . .

# Dietary Therapy Appears to Help Multiple Sclerosis Patients

## Zoltan P. Rona

Multiple sclerosis is a disease that has no cure but many treatments. Not all are accepted by the medical establishment, however. In the following viewpoint a doctor who advocates alternative therapies touts the benefits of nutritional therapies for multiple sclerosis patients. Zoltan P. Rona acknowledges that most experts dismiss dietary treatment for MS, but he claims that they are overlooking the benefits of various therapies. Vitamin $B_{12}$, which occurs naturally in meat and dairy products, has produced positive results in many MS patients, Rona states. Treatment of food allergies can also reduce MS symptoms, he says. Various nutritional supplements, such as fish oil, are also valuable treatments, according to the Canadian holistic practitioner. Rona graduated from the McGill University Medical School and holds a master's degree in biochemistry and clinical nutrition from the University of Bridgeport in Connecticut. He is past president of the Canadian Holistic Medical Association. His Web site is www.mydoctor.ca/drzoltanrona.

**SOURCE:** Zoltan P. Rona, "Multiple Sclerosis and Natural Therapies," *HealthLink*, 2008. Reproduced by permission of the author.

Multiple sclerosis is a disease that affects different parts of the nervous system through the destruction of the myelin sheaths, the structures that cover the nerves. The inflammatory response produces any number of symptoms including blurred vision, staggering gait, numbness, dizziness, tremors, slurred speech, bowel and bladder problems, sexual impotence in men and paralysis.

MS usually occurs in persons between the ages of twenty-five and forty. The disease may disappear for long periods of time, then return with acute symptom flare-ups. It progresses slowly and may last several decades in many cases. On the other hand, in a minority, it can develop rapidly and progress unremittingly to death. There

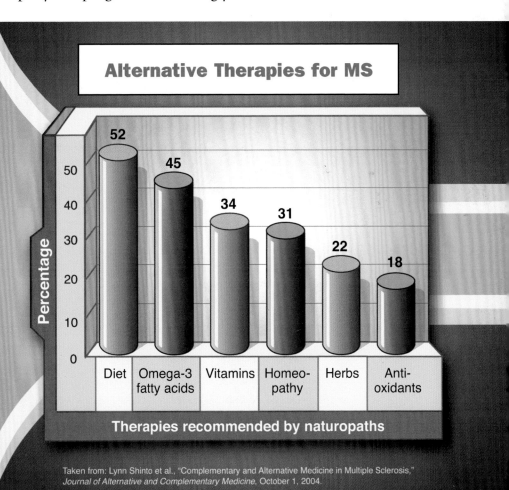

**Alternative Therapies for MS**

Taken from: Lynn Shinto et al., "Complementary and Alternative Medicine in Multiple Sclerosis," *Journal of Alternative and Complementary Medicine*, October 1, 2004.

is no universally accepted treatment for MS. ACTH (hormone) injections are often used in acute exacerbations, as are immunosuppressive drugs. These, of course, have severe side effects. When asked about the role of nutrition in MS, most conventional medical doctors still claim there is no benefit to any diet changes. I disagree.

### Virtues of B$_{12}$

Although the definitive cause of MS is unknown, a growing number of scientific studies suggest that nutrition may be a very important factor. Nutrition oriented health care practitioners have noticed that early MS can be helped by optimizing nutritional status with respect to essential fatty acids, amino acids, minerals such as zinc, selenium and magnesium and B vitamins, especially vitamin B$_{12}$ and folic acid.

**FAST FACT**

Two small studies have shown weak but encouraging evidence that multiple sclerosis patients benefit from the omega-3 fatty acid in fish oil.

In my practice, I have noted tremendous subjective improvements in many MS patients after a series of vitamin B$_{12}$ and folic acid injections. Not only did all these patients have greater energy after vitamin B$_{12}$ and folic acid treatments, but, objectively, there were improvements in nerve conduction studies done by neurologists. Spontaneous remission? Not likely because both vitamins have been demonstrated to improve nerve cell function. It is indeed possible that some cases of MS are really B vitamin deficiencies in disguise.

Most cases of MS (over 80% according to one 25 year study) improve on a low saturated fat diet. Researchers have also reported that symptoms improve when food intolerances (allergies) are eliminated. In my experience, the commonest hidden food allergies appear to be wheat, milk, eggs, yeast and corn. Testing and treatment of these allergies may unlock the door to recovery for many MS sufferers.

## Supplements May Help

Supplements which are very effective in both prevention and treatment of MS include fish oil (omega-3-EPA) and evening primrose oil capsules. Dosages depend on the severity of the illness and the patient's tolerance for these supplements. Alternatives include flaxseed oil, edible linseed oil, oil of borage and black currant oil. Vitamin E and other antioxidants (vitamin A, beta carotene, B complex vitamins, vitamin C, vitamin $D_3$, zinc, selenium, pycnogenol and others) are also beneficial.

Hypersensitivity to toxic heavy metals such as mercury can produce all the symptoms of MS. So can Lyme Disease. Testing for these two possibilities is certainly worth while. Some dentists have advocated the replacement of all mercury dental fillings with non-metal fillings as a therapy for MS. Although the testimonials that support the replacement of the common mercury filling in MS patients are legion, it is still a highly controversial topic. In my practice, I have had at least a dozen MS victims improve drastically after replacement of mercury

Some alternative practitioners claim that fish oil supplements can both treat and prevent multiple sclerosis. (Image copyright Alan Eddinton, 2009. Used under license from Shutterstock.com.)

dental fillings. Unfortunately, an equal number have had no change in their health status as a result of this sort of treatment. Hair mineral analysis and urine tests can screen for excess body burdens of mercury as well as other toxic heavy metals that may interfere with the immune system. High levels can usually be offset by supplementation with vitamin C, selenium, garlic, cysteine, methionine and other high sulfur containing compounds. . . .

Some authors also believe that MS can be benefited by anti-candida [yeast infection] treatment. This too is controversial. In situations where all else has failed and the patient is in the early stages of the disease, trial therapy with a yeast-free diet and natural antifungal remedies may be warranted.

# Dietary Therapy Remains Unproven for Multiple Sclerosis

## Institute of Medicine

The following viewpoint is a list of popular dietary therapies for multiple sclerosis and a critique of each. Coming from the Institute of Medicine of the National Academy of Sciences, the critique carries the weight of a widely acknowledged authority. The Institute of Medicine's committee on multiple sclerosis finds no proven merit in any of the dozens of alternative remedies. In some cases, it warns of dangers either to the pocketbook or the body in the proposed treatment. Taken altogether, the list comprises an indictment of the widespread practice in alternative medicine of marketing supposed therapies without first completing rigorous studies to establish their safety and effectiveness. The Institute of Medicine was chartered in 1970 as a branch of the National Academy of Sciences to provide science-based advice on matters of biomedical science.

Treatments That Have Been Claimed to Be of Benefit in MS:

*Allergen-Free Diet.* Regular use of a diet from which foods are eliminated that are known to produce hives, other skin eruptions, asthmatic attacks, and so on. There is no relationship of MS [multiple sclerosis] to external allergens demonstrated. The diet has not been shown to be effective and has dropped out of favor.

*Kousmine Diet.* A low-fat, low-concentrated sugar, high-fiber diet, supplemented by vitamins A, D, E, C, and B complex. There is no scientific evidence that this particular dietary method is effective in treating MS.

*Gluten-Free Diet.* A balanced diet excluding wheat and rye. This diet must be considered ineffective in MS.

Scientists at the Institute of Medicine of the National Academy of Sciences say that many alternative remedies have not proved to be effective in treating MS and, in fact, may even be harmful. (© **Digital Vision Ltd./Super Stock**)

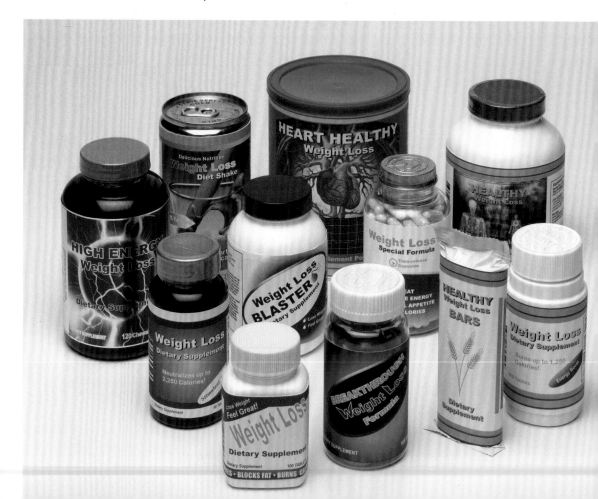

*Raw Food, Evers Diet.* A diet containing only natural (unprocessed) foods, including a daily intake of germinated wheat. It appears that this diet should be considered ineffective in MS.

*MacDougal Diet.* This diet combines a low-fat diet with a gluten-free diet and adds supplements of vitamins and minerals. There is no scientific evidence that this diet is effective in MS.

*Pectin- and Fructose-Restricted Diet.* A diet from which unripe fruits, fruit juices, and pectin-containing fruits and vegetables are eliminated, supplemented with menadione (vitamin $K_3$). The methanol hypothesis and the dietary regimen based on it remain unproven.

> **FAST FACT**
>
> Melatonin is promoted to some MS patients, but some studies indicate it may actually worsen the symptoms of MS.

*Cambridge and Other Liquid Diets.* A balanced, very low-calorie liquid, used in the treatment of obesity. Calorie intake is 330/day with a suboptimal level of protein at 22 g [grams]/day. Extra potassium is supplied. This diet is not recommended for the treatment of MS.

*Sucrose- and Tobacco-Free Diet.* Elimination of all food products containing sucrose in the form of cane, brown, or maple sugars, molasses, sorghum, or dates; also products containing propylene glycol or glycol stearate. Tobacco is not to be used in any form. This therapy remains unproven.

*Vitamins.* Individual vitamins or combinations of vitamins are taken in capsule or liquid form as a supplement to a normal diet. Adequate intake of vitamins is advised in all patients with MS, but there appears to be no scientific proof that supplementary doses of vitamins, alone or in combination, favorably affect the course of this disease.

*Megavitamin Therapy.* Massive doses of vitamins. There appears to be no reliable evidence that megavitamin therapy influences the course of MS.

*Megascorbic Therapy.* Massive doses of vitamin C (ascorbic acid), referred to as an orthomolecular treatment. The value of megascorbic therapy in MS is unproven and this treatment is not recommended.

*Minerals.* Addition of various mineral salts to diet. There appears to be no clear evidence that any of these regimens should be considered effective in MS.

*Cerebrosides.* Dietary supplementation with fatty acids of cerebrosides from beef spinal cord. On the basis of published evidence, this treatment is considered ineffective in MS.

*Aloe Vera.* Juice of the aloe vera plant, available over-the-counter, taken by mouth on regular basis. Aloe vera is not recommended for use in MS.

*Enzymes.* A diet similar to the Evers diet, supplemented with plant and bacterial enzymes, normal digestive enzymes, vitamins, and minerals, lipolytic enzymes, and others. Enzyme supplementation is not recommended.

*St. John's Wort.* This plant has been used for hundreds of years and has recently been popularized as a treatment for many conditions. The active ingredient is hypericum. St. John's Wort [taken by mouth] can be helpful in mild depression. If depression is severe or protracted, standard antidepressants should be used. In the opinion of the committee, St. John's Wort is not a treatment for MS, but might be beneficial in patients who have mild depression or mood change.

*Oral Calcium + Magnesium + Vitamin D.* Inexpensive chemicals available commercially, taken by mouth. The efficacy of this treatment is yet to be determined.

*Hyperimmune Colostrum (Immune Milk).* Pregnant cows are inoculated with measles vaccine or other viruses considered to be related to MS. Colostrum (early milk) is frozen for preservation and taken by mouth. This treatment remains unproven and is not recommended. A clinical trial of adequate size would be required to determine whether it has any value.

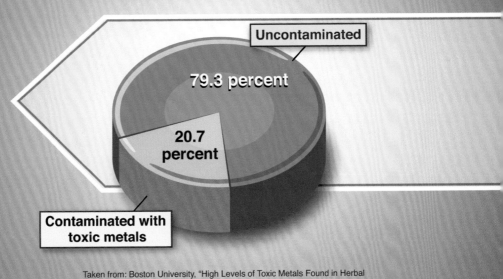

## Herbal Medicines Often Contain Dangerous Impurities

Sample of ayurvedic herbal medicines sold on the Internet:

**Uncontaminated**

79.3 percent

20.7 percent

**Contaminated with toxic metals**

Taken from: Boston University, "High Levels of Toxic Metals Found in Herbal Medicine Products Sold Online," *Science Daily*, August 27, 2008.

*Metabolic Therapy.* A complex program of regimens and medications said to affect mineral balance, diet, and bowel function, e.g., alkalinity of the small intestine; also immune colostrum and high doses of vitamin C, SOD [superoxide dismutase], vitamin A, "thymotropic" tablets to stimulate the immune system, octacosanol, B complex vitamins. This is an unproven, expensive, and possibly dangerous procedure with no known scientific basis. . . .

*Honey Bee Venom.* Extracts of the bee venom. There are no objective controlled studies. Based on the evidence, this treatment is not recommended. The Committee feels that there is no generally accepted scientific basis for use of this therapy because it never has been tested in a properly controlled trial, and its use carries significant risk. . . .

*Cellular Therapy.* Injection of ground-up brain or other tissues freshly prepared from unborn calves, lambs, or pigs. The little published information suggests that this treatment should be considered ineffective in MS and potentially dangerous.

# CHAPTER 3

# Experiences with Multiple Sclerosis

# Falling Out
# of the Closet

## David L. Lander

For an actor, a loss of mobility raises fears of a suddenly terminated career. In the following viewpoint David L. Lander tells of his experience playing the character Squiggy in the highly popular TV series *Laverne and Shirley* while trying to conceal what to him was a terrible secret: He had been diagnosed with multiple sclerosis. Like many people with the disease, it took Lander quite a while to figure out that something was seriously wrong. He would have little episodes, and when they began to add up, he wondered if he had a mental problem. Only after landing in the hospital did he receive a diagnosis of MS. At that point, he put out a cover story and kept his disease secret for more than a decade. Lander trained as an actor and comedian at Carnegie Mellon University. After going public with his disease, Lander became a goodwill ambassador for the National Multiple Sclerosis Society.

*Photo on facing page.*
A woman with multiple sclerosis gets help gripping the pool ladder during swimming physiotherapy.
(© Marina Dempster/ First Light/Alamy)

**SOURCE:** David L. Lander, *Fall Down Laughing: How Squiggy Caught Multiple Sclerosis and Didn't Tell Nobody.* New York: Jeremy P. Tarcher/Putnam, 2000. Copyright © 2000 by David L. Lander. All rights reserved. Used by permission of Jeremy P. Tarcher, an imprint of Penguin Group (USA) Inc.

Until last May [1999], I was best known as Squiggy on the TV sitcom *Laverne & Shirley*. But then I told *People* magazine and anyone else who would listen that for the last fifteen years I've had multiple sclerosis. During my silent years, between 1984 and 1999, I continued working in Hollywood while hiding the symptoms of my illness. I did voice-overs for various cartoons and animated feature films, played supporting roles in a dozen movies and was a regular on a handful of television series, including *On the Air, Twin Peaks,* and *Pacific Blue.*

In my real life, I somehow managed to stay married to the same wonderful woman for twenty-one years. Today, we live in a suburb outside of Los Angeles with our seventeen-year-old daughter who has never known her father without MS.

At the time of my diagnosis, I had just turned thirty-six and was coming off seven years on *Laverne & Shirley.* I was five years into my marriage with Kathy Fields; our daughter, Natalie, had just had her first birthday. The biggest problems of the moment were actor problems, not real-life problems. I was trying to break out of being typecast as Squiggy, a role I loved, but one I needed to move beyond. Before that, I had had a ten-year history as a writer and actor who did comedy on radio, television, and in clubs. I was confident of my future, and was beginning to branch out. I was developing a new television series, writing a film script for [the Hollywood studio] MGM, and performing supporting roles in a few major films.

## Puzzling Signs

Like everyone with MS, there were clues that something was wrong with me but nothing added up as remarkable. Symptoms appeared and disappeared as if by magic; slowly, little by little, inch by inch. I would step in holes that were not there, trip on cracks in the sidewalk, or watch a drink slip through my hands twice in one night without feeling it leave my fingertips.

It seemed like my body was out of sync, like a badly dubbed Hercules picture. I could no longer trust it to follow the simplest instructions. On some days, crossing streets and climbing curbs became a challenge. On other days I would be okay. I knew something wasn't right,

Actor and viewpoint author David L. Lander appeared as Squiggy on the hit TV series *Laverne and Shirley*. He went public about having MS and, in an effort to raise awareness about the disease, became an ambassador for the National Multiple Sclerosis Society. **(Mike Guastella/ WireImage)**

FAST FACT

Teri Garr, Lena Horne, and the late Richard Pryor are just some of the famous performers who have coped with MS.

I just didn't know what it was called, if it was serious, or if it would ever go away.

On the days my body didn't listen, I told myself it was just one of those days, I didn't know what "one of those days" meant; nothing hurt, my body just wasn't working like it should. Then, without warning, I'd feel normal again. It was like living on a fault line. I knew a quake was coming, but I didn't know when it would erupt or how big the quake would be.

Nothing made sense. I had begun to doubt my experience of what was happening. I thought maybe I had become a hypochondriac, or just losing my mind. . . .

## Diagnosis Made

When I was still emerging from a fog of anesthesia, Kathy and the neurologist stood as unsteady blurs at my bedside and delivered the news. *"You have multiple sclerosis."* The words sounded strange. I repeated them silently. It was unlikely that I would be able to walk again, the doctor said, and if I did, it wouldn't be for long. High doses of steroids might help in the short term. But in the end, the only thing I could count on was that the disease would progress. I would get worse.

My legs lay still, completely numb from the spinal tap. The information the doctor had just given me was not sinking in. It hovered in the air, separate and incomprehensible. Worst-case scenarios circled. In my mind's eye, I saw [actors] Lionel Barrymore in *It's a Wonderful Life* and Raymond Burr in *Ironside*, both in wheelchairs and hooked up to iron lungs. I turned away from the doctor and looked out the window of my room, located in a wing of private rooms on the top floor of one of the towers at Cedars Sinai Hospital. I could see only blue sky and the silhouette of another hospital tower. The doctor droned on about all the horrible things I would look forward to and I thought, *Talk about bedside manner. Frankly, Doctor, I am not impressed.*

## A Death Nearby

Later that afternoon, an Associated Press reporter called from the hospital lobby to find out why I was in the hospital. I tried to convince him that in fact *he* was in the hospital and I was downstairs but to no avail. He then asked what was really on his mind—Did I know anything about [comic actor] Andy Kaufman?

"What about him?" I asked.

"He just died in the room next door."

"Of what?" I asked. "Andy was a little crazy but he didn't do drugs or anything that would make him die."

Later that night, my general practitioner, Dr. Kipper, stopped by for a visit. He had also been Andy Kaufman's doctor, and he told me Andy *had* died earlier in the day in the room next door.

I looked at Kipper and thought, *What kind of hospital is this? I have MS and Andy Kaufman is dead?* It was all too strange. I didn't understand. "Andy was crazy," I told Kipper, "but you don't die of crazy."

"No you don't," Kipper agreed. "You die of cancer."

## Cover Story

Cedars Sinai was crawling with reporters hunting for information about Kaufman. They and everyone else in the hospital seemed stunned. My friends came in and out of my room shaking their heads about the news. Like the rest of the world, none of us had known Andy was sick.

And I had my own problems. I could empathize with Kaufman's reticence. After all, I, too, was in the hospital with a potentially life-threatening disease, and I was lying to everyone in sight about it.

When friends Michael McKean, Harry Shearer, and my writing partners, Peter Elbling and Garry Goodrow visited, I told them it was a bad disk. I remember looking at Peter and Garry one afternoon. We had spent the last month working on a pilot script for my new show. "Hey, fellas," I wanted to ask them, "how do you think it would play if my character was in a wheelchair?"

For the five days I was in the hospital, it seemed as though every time I turned on the television all I saw were actors running. (Since when did actors run everywhere?) I saw them jogging on beautiful beaches, sprint in hot pursuit of a bad guy, chase after their dog in the park on a crisp autumn day. No one seemed to walk from place to place anymore—let alone get *wheeled* around.

Everyone bought my bad-disk story, though Shearer did not believe the truthful news of Kaufman's death. Like many, he was convinced that Andy was alive and well, and the death was feigned—one of Kaufman's wild pranks. "No," I told Harry. "It's not, it's real. He's really dead." . . .

## Swift Recovery

By the middle of my first night in the hospital, I was able to walk again. I had called for the nurse and when she didn't come, I pulled myself out of bed and walked to the bathroom. I was amazed! Twelve hours of intravenous Prednisone were miraculous. By the following day, I felt almost normal. I could still walk, and my legs felt strong enough that if I didn't know better, I could have sworn it was all a bad dream. Of course, I could never forget the truth. But the steroids worked so well that it was easy to imagine I might have miraculously gotten better. I kept reminding myself that what I had was incurable, but it was tough to keep fooling myself when Dr. Kipper kept saying that he had never seen such a fast recovery.

That's how it works in the wonderful world of MS— an illness that affects everyone differently. The only typical experience of most people with MS is what's known as an exacerbation or attack. Anything can set one off, including heat, stress, physical or emotional trauma, or any infection like a cold. But scientists maintain what's most notable about MS flare-ups are their unpredictable nature. Sometimes, an exacerbation can be caused by nothing at all.

## Mobility Comes and Goes

After each flare-up, though, the progress of the disease can worsen. The cells attack the nerve myelin and sometimes the damage is extensive; other times it's not. When I have flare-ups, my legs buckle and I fall down. I often have other symptoms—weakness that leads to drop foot —the inability to lift my foot high enough to prevent tripping when walking—balance disorientation, and numbing of my hands and feet—I am so far a lucky guy: after each flare-up I have recovered without losing too much mobility.

While today I accept the unpredictability of living with flare-ups, in the beginning, I had no idea what to expect. Nobody else did, either. The professionals in my life took on the roles of good doc, bad doc. My first neurologist focused on the worst-case scenario by telling me I would not be able to walk. Kipper focused on the best-case scenario by insisting that flare-ups might be infrequent. Neither turned out to be right, but of the two, all my bets were on Kipper. He bucked me up at a critical time. I thought that maybe the worst had happened and maybe I could go on and live with a disease like MS. Maybe I would be one of those people who had this terrible experience and would never have it again? They even had a name for it. "Singular sclerosis." That's what I wanted: in and out sclerosis.

This was where I placed my focus—on a happy ending. I didn't want people comparing me to anyone else they knew who had been laid low by MS. Whoever they had in mind, it wasn't going to be me! I needed to believe that I was going to be one of the lucky ones, and for a while, I was.

## Hooked on Steroids

When I got out of the hospital, I continued on steroids for four months. At first I was given very high doses intravenously which were followed by a tapering oral dose. I remember going to Peter Elbling's house to finish writing a pilot, and downing huge handfuls of prednisone pills. This was my wonder drug. As long as I took it, my MS was controlled.

But high doses of steroids have their downside and as time went on, I developed a love/hate relationship with the drug. I'd go around euphoric and smiling. Then an hour later, I'd get mad at a busy signal on the phone. I was impossible to live with. On steroids, intense feelings of well-being are followed by impatience, restlessness, and anger. *But I need it!* At times, I hated myself for becoming dependent on the prednisone. I lost patience with my family. I lost patience with life. Emotionally, it rocked me. And physically it made my skin break out and my face puff up. I grew sad and bloated, but the drug worked miracles. When I was on it, I could do whatever I wanted and whatever was asked of me.

Despite my good reaction to steroid therapy, my first neurologist had said that it would only be a matter of time before other symptoms would arise. Based on the location of the sclerosis, he outlined future possible symptoms in great detail: dizziness and vertigo; mood swings; loss of hand dexterity; coordination difficulties and muscle stiffness and weakness; speech and voice impediments; memory loss and drop foot. His words haunted me, and I spent my idle time asking myself the same question—how much longer would I be able to walk? And as much as I wanted to believe that I was destined to have a miracle recovery from MS, by the time I was diagnosed, I had already had several exacerbations. I didn't know what they were then; I just knew that I fell down a lot. My legs would grow weak, as if someone had taken the air out of my tires, and when I was tired, I often lost my balance.

## Pants Tell the Tale

Once I understood what these episodes were, I figured out that I could always tell what was going on with my MS by looking at my pants. At any given time, I could walk to my closet and find four pairs with a hole in the right knee. *That was at the ballpark and that one over there was in June on the stairs.* Falling down happened so often that when I felt myself begin to lose my balance, I would yell, "Excuse me." Thud. "Damn, there goes another pair of pants."

# Seeing a Life Above Illness

## Richard M. Cohen

When Richard M. Cohen was just twenty-five years old, multiple sclerosis struck. In the following viewpoint he discusses how, as a young television news producer with expectations of a limitless future, he suddenly lost sight in one eye. This ominous development was the herald of a lifetime with MS. Like many people, Cohen could not accept the diagnosis that followed and simply tried to live as he had before. However, as his doctors had predicted, the symptoms of multiple sclerosis returned. Cohen battled on, taking massive amounts of steroids in an attempt to stave them off. The steroids played havoc with his mind and body, and eventually their beneficial effect on the MS symptoms wore off. Eventually, Cohen was forced to admit to his boss, ABC News legend Ted Koppel, that he had MS. Coming clean was the first step in learning to cope, Cohen says, but he still had a long and hard road ahead of him. Despite battling MS since 1973, TV news producer Cohen has won three Emmy Awards for his work.

**SOURCE:** Richard M. Cohen, *Blindsided: Lifting a Life Above Illness: A Reluctant Memoir.* New York: HarperCollins, 2004. Copyright © 2004 by Richard M. Cohen. All rights reserved. Reproduced by permission of HarperCollins Publishers, Inc.

On a chilly morning in October 1973, my eyes flickered open as the sun was rising and horror hit like lightning, lifting me up out of bed, stunned and standing motionless next to the window. I was blind in my right eye. Blind. Totally sightless. The usual early morning routine of coffee and newspapers in a sunny kitchen was replaced by my own dark headline. I stood, softly mumbling to the empty room, "No. This is not happening."

The videotape in my mind kept replaying. The day before had begun normally. I had been feeling good, living without any of the symptoms of multiple sclerosis I had first experienced since the diagnosis was imposed only four months earlier. But sometime in the morning, a tiny spot, an oil slick on my right eye, just a speck, had suddenly appeared. That spot was a little round puddle that could not be rubbed away, pooling on my window to the world. An afternoon had been spent opening and closing both eyes, hoping to tear up and wash the nuisance away.

Now I was blind. Losing the sight of one eye is a classic manifestation of multiple sclerosis. Even I knew that. As I stood by the bed, wobbling in that chilly bedroom, toes gripping the floor, the terrible truth washed over me. For months I had lived in a house of denial. Now, in one moment, it had given way. It had been a flimsy structure, built on wishful thinking, but it had sheltered me from the heavy weight of a reality I could not bear to confront. Ignorance had been my ally; I had not even asked many questions of the doctors. Silence was an odd tactic for a journalist who, by trade, is all questions all the time. But I did not want to know too many facts. Facts would lead to truth, and truth had been unacceptable. I was facing facts now. I had to admit to myself that I had MS.

## Lengthy Denial

Years would pass, however, before I easily and openly acknowledged my illness. Knowledge came slowly, too.

## FAST FACT

About half of the people with relapsing-remitting MS have optic neuritis (visual impairment) as their first symptom.

I had much to understand about multiple sclerosis, an illness that was then, and even now, little understood. MS is a disease with no sure treatment and no certain outcomes, no cures and no definitive cause. Some experts suspect a virus, others environmental factors. Some think that the human immune system, the body's defense against invading germs and microbes, can be so effective that it occasionally turns on the body itself. And the idea of a genetic component lay far in the future. Finally, I had been drafted, only this time into the army of 350,000 Americans who shadowbox with this neurological enemy they cannot see.

What is evident is that multiple sclerosis is a disease of process, a grim pileup on the highways of the central nervous system. Multiple patches of plaque form where the disease hits motor and sensory nerves after the protective myelin sheath peels away. The illness process is similar to an attack on an old-fashioned telephone switchboard, with its insulation pulling away, short-circuiting phone calls. Signals cross. Life is disrupted. Dreams are derailed.

### Warnings Come True

"Watch out" is what the doctors had been telling me since the diagnosis was pronounced. But because no one could tell me just how my life would change—MS's effects are not uniformly predictable—I had refused to take their warnings seriously. Now my life was disrupted. Big time.

I entered the hospital reluctantly, my bravado in the dust. The primitive procedures began. Drugs were dispensed with no certain knowledge that they necessarily helped. I endured regular steroid drips, pumped into my arms four times each day. The steroids wreaked havoc on my body, triggering mood swings and, ultimately, depression. "The treatment will kill you if the MS doesn't," a nurse joked.

I gained almost fifty pounds because my appetite and metabolism were thrown off. Some eyesight was restored, a partial remission, but not enough to approach normalcy. Desperation drove me to allow residents to experiment on me, injecting the powerful steroids through my lower eyelid and under the eye itself, a barbaric attempt to reach the damaged optic nerve. I must have been crazy. I visualized the young doctors jumping up and down, squealing in delight, "Oh boy, let's try this now." I was learning to dislike doctors. They treated me as an inanimate object. Through the years, I have elevated that antipathy to an art form.

## Revealing the Truth

The next step on the road to reality came with a call from Ted Koppel, my senior colleague at ABC News. Ted had traveled to China with President Nixon on that historic 1972 trip and was in the Asian nation again on assignment. Since a correspondent on the ground in a closed society would likely be the last to know about major events within those borders, we had arranged a system for me to check regularly with a State Department source about Chinese political and military activity. Ted was to call me from China, and I would feed him whatever information I had picked up, disguised, thinly no doubt, as casual conversation.

When Ted's next call from Beijing came, it was rerouted by the ABC switchboard to a number I had given the operators. Our routine conversation about China became an awkward high-volume question-and-answer session about why I was in Georgetown Hospital. "What the hell are you doing there? What is wrong?" Ted asked.

Silence. I did not know what to say. Should I just tell the truth? Nobody at ABC knew anything about my illness or whereabouts. I remember hearing faint, scratchy voices in the distance, jabbering in Chinese, while I was

Viewpoint author Richard M. Cohen has lived with MS since 1973. (Brendan Hoffman/Getty Images)

thinking hard about what my response to Ted should be. "I have MS," I finally said softly.

## Being Heard

"You have what?" Ted shouted. He must have thought I was referring to MSG, maybe trying to order takeout from him. "Hello? Cohen, I still cannot hear you," he yelled through the phone, knocking me back onto the bed. Phone calls from China were patched though many relay points thirty years ago. "I said I have multiple sclerosis," I yelled back. "Are you deaf?"

The silence grew briefly louder. "I heard you," he said. "Stop shouting." Ted paused. "Take care of yourself." Done. I was out of the closet. With that information, shouted across oceans and continents, crossing

PERSPECTIVES ON DISEASES AND DISORDERS

political and emotional borders, I finally sealed to myself that I truly did have this serious disease.

Candor had become my first exercise in coping. Open, free-flowing honesty was moving slowly but trickling out, first to myself and then to another. The flow could not be reversed. I knew that. Coping can be a complicated mind game. My life lay before me. I needed some time to figure the new realities out.

## Confidence Sapped

My image of self was involuntarily being altered. The person painfully squinting and looking out from the mirror was changing before my eyes. I could see neither this stranger nor the mirror with clarity. I felt powerless, a passenger in a speeding car, the automatic transmission whirring on the steep climb. I was shifting gears, barely aware of the strains of this new uphill adventure.

Change was profound, the loss of control unnerving. Anyone's early years out of school and in the world are all about empowerment. My sense of strength had grown as fast as bamboo. Confidence in the future suddenly was neutralized. The certainty of success had cracked because it was clear now that this illness was going to touch everything that I did from now on. There was no confidence that my vision would return, intact. And it would not. This was going to be a new world for me.

The signs were everywhere. I was unsteady on my feet, bumping into people and furniture, glancing off doorways and tripping on stairs. A lady in the hospital pulled out a cigarette as she sat with guests in the designated visiting area near the elevators (smoking in hospitals was astonishingly common then). I lit a match and went to touch it to her cigarette. I missed by six inches because my lateral perception was so damaged. The lady laughed at me, and I shrank back.

The range of horrors that could become the future was flashing before me. I was staring at the twisted mirrors in the fun house and not having a good time. Damaged goods had replaced the label *winner*. I would be a limited person.

## Brain Tumor Threat

And the beat went on. At one point, doctors thought I might have a brain tumor because of an ambiguous brain scan. Wasn't MS enough? I was fast learning that things always can be worse, an observation that would serve me well in the future. I was strapped down as pressure injections forced dye into my brain in a now abandoned procedure called an arteriogram. A young nurse held my head in her arms. The test was negative, but I was positive my head would explode. The pain and pressure were greater than anything I have experienced in the thirty years since.

Another small epiphany came. Human endurance is of a vast proportion that most of us do not realize. We think we are weak, failing to recognize our intrinsic strength. I was stronger than ever I realized.

In the midst of this chaos in the clinic, Republican lawyers from the Watergate Committee came looking for me, intent on getting information about an ill-conceived campaign espionage plan in George McGovern's 1972 presidential campaign. McGovern's handlers had wanted to steal me away from ABC to spy on Vice President Agnew. This was before satellites and the era of instant communication, and the McGovern people wanted eyes and ears on the Agnew campaign. The plan had died the death of a bad idea. Now the Republicans were looking for ammunition to fire back at the Democrats.

## Feeling Punished

Events in my life were spinning out of control, even as I was desperately attempting to ground myself in new circumstances. I knew the McGovern thing had been crazy. It would have been an adventure. Composing affidavits now in a hospital room and all the pressure only confused me. Was I being punished for something?

The emotional artillery was out and thundering. I was squirming, finding it difficult to duck while lying in prone position, flat out in a hospital bed. Tethered by tubes, I could not head for any fire exit and run, screaming into the distance. I was stuck with myself. Such thoughts ran through my head in every waking hour, or at least in lucid moments. Much of the time I just lay there, pumped with industrial-strength steroids, additional assorted drugs, and heavy pain medication that dispatched me to La-La Land.

Hey, wait a minute, I bellowed in my head. Stop the show. I'm only twenty-five. I don't need this. I'm out of here. Not so fast, reality answered.

# Climbing the Mountain

## Wendy Booker, interviewed by Taryn Plumb

The prospect of scaling a mountain is daunting enough for the average person. For a multiple sclerosis patient, it might well seem impossible. No so for Wendy Booker. In the following viewpoint the fifty-two-year-old New Hampshire native says she aims to become the face of MS by demonstrating the will to conquer through her mountain-climbing achievements. In particular, she has set herself the goal of climbing the world's most formidable peaks. She has already scaled four of the world's seven highest mountains. Her quest is to conquer them all by 2009, ending with the tallest and deadliest peak in the world, Mount Everest. A decade after her diagnosis, Booker—a former interior decorator—is now one of the most famous and accomplished MS patients in the world. Taryn Plumb is a professional journalist based in New York.

T he climb is slow and severe, a solitary creep up snowy crevasses and across 18-inch ridges that drop into oblivion.

SOURCE: Taryn Plumb, "No Mountain High Enough," *Boston Globe*, January 21, 2007. Reproduced by permission of the author.

There are altitude headaches. Burning eyes. She cries because it hurts, because the white slopes seem to stretch forever into the clouds. Sometimes it's hard to breathe. Other times, she just wants her mother.

Separated from other hikers by 20-foot lengths of rope, Wendy Booker endures by recalling trips to Moscow with her sons or chewing gummy bears. Numbers and calculations run like code through her head. Upbeat songs serve as a soundtrack on an iPod.

"It's like doing a marathon every day," explained Booker, a Manchester native with multiple sclerosis who has climbed the four highest peaks on four continents. "You have to go someplace where you can say, 'I can put up with this.' Anything to keep you going."

## Joining the Few

They are hulking, relentless beasts, gruff and temperamental; deadly for some. Known as the Seven Summits, they represent the loftiest pinnacles on each continent. A small number of people—barely more than 100—have reached the top of every one.

Booker wants to be the first woman with MS to scale them all. It's the 52-year-old's quest to beat back her illness, to defy it.

"Don't let the disease define you," she said, wiping at wet eyes as she sat in her Manchester apartment, on the second floor of a red, cedar-shingle house with a rusty cricket weathervane. Nearby, sliding glass doors offered a view of the inner harbor and two white-steepled churches. "That's become my entire mission. I want to be the face of MS."

The former interior designer and single mother of three sons was diagnosed nine years ago; the disease has left her numb on her left side, from the tips of her toes to her rib cage. She walks with the slightest limp, and also experiences dizziness, vision, and balance disturbances.

## Redefining Limits

Considering those restrictions, she uses the mountains as a metaphor for the illness and the human will—but also to offer a more realistic perception of MS.

Most often, the autoimmune disease—which affects the central nervous system of roughly 400,000 people nationwide—is associated with spasms, paralysis, and blindness, she said. Hardly ever do people envision a trim, blond, 50ish woman traversing steep ice faces or sleeping in a tent on a mountainside.

She's a radical example, of course. She'll even use words like "crazy" to describe the challenge she's taken on. Like many athletes, though, she's compelled by an impalpable force, addicted to the strategy, unpredictability, and perseverance that come with mountain climbing.

It became an all-consuming quest in 2002, after weather steered her off a recreational climb on Alaska's Mount McKinley. She quit her job to train full time, and sought sponsorship for the mountains from Teva Pharmaceutical Industries Ltd., which provides her with daily injections of [the prescription drug] Copaxone to battle MS symptoms.

She now has just three more summits to go, having just this month [January 2007] conquered South America's Aconcagua. [She climbed] Antarctica's Vinson [in January 2008]. Kosciuszko, in Australia, [was summited by Booker in November 2008]. Everest, the big one, is the challenge for 2009.

When she's not struggling up icy peaks, Booker is a motivational speaker. Last year [2006], she did nearly 70 talks across the country. Her message: Climb your own mountains.

"Just because you don't get to the top, doesn't mean you're not good enough," she said in an interview pre-

> **FAST FACT**
>
> A survey of people with multiple sclerosis reveals that 94 percent find it at least somewhat disruptive in their overall daily life, and 64 percent experience difficulty walking or cannot walk at all.

Aconcagua, bustling between suitcase-stuffing, cellphone calls, and the delivery of a satellite phone for mountain-top communication. "It'll still be there tomorrow.". . .

## Marathon Led to Mountains

Nine years ago, though, she wasn't thinking about mountaintops or strategic ways to traverse them. She just envisioned a wheelchair.

Zoe Koplowitz, a fifty-six-year-old afflicted with MS, finishes her seventeenth New York City marathon in twenty-nine hours and fifteen minutes. The author says MS sufferers should challenge themselves physically to overcome the disease. (**AP Images**)

She was diagnosed in 1998, after experiencing numbness in her left leg. Initially, she had what she called a "pity party," and feared she'd lose all sensation in her legs.

But then she did something extraordinary: Knowing exercise was crucial to battling MS, she ran the Boston Marathon. After that, she just wanted to go bigger and higher.

"I really made mountain climbing my prime objective," she said.

But to bump into her on the street, you'd never imagine she's dug her ice ax into 20,000-foot peaks. She's trim but not immaculately chiseled, toned but not a vein-bulging, zero-body-fat specimen.

Mountain climbers are very rarely distinguishable in build, noted Booker's trainer, Catherine Sullivan of Beverly. Their goals are endurance and stamina, not girth or sheer strength. She guides Booker in "functional" exercises with weights and cardio three times a week. In preparation for a climb, Booker will strap on a pack filled with 45 pounds of sunflower seeds and set the treadmill to its highest altitude.

She runs six times a week, too, and does marathons between climbs. She's completed nine, five of them in Boston. . . .

## Overcoming Fear

It's about fighting back fear, too, Booker explained. People die all the time on these peaks—Everest alone claimed about 15 last year—but she doesn't let that overwhelm her.

"People say, 'Aren't you scared?' I just can't live that way, always worried about the future. Do I get afraid sometimes? Oh, you bet."

Especially when it comes to Everest. To prepare, she'll climb Cho Oyu in the Himalayas, a common training ground for those with eyes on the big daddy of all mountains, because it's similar in altitude and terrain. She also plans to move to Boulder, Colo., to acclimate to a higher altitude.

"I have a lot of respect for the mountain, and when I do it, I'm going to be ready for it, mentally and physically," she said. "I have to wrap my head around it."

And after Everest?

"I get post-event letdown," she said with a laugh, "I don't know—the space shuttle?"

# GLOSSARY

| | |
|---|---|
| **activities of daily living (ADL)** | Everyday routines generally involving functional mobility and personal care, such as bathing, dressing, toileting, and meal preparation. An inability to perform these due to multiple sclerosis renders a person dependent on others. |
| **antibodies** | Special Y-shaped proteins produced by immune system cells that circulate in the blood until they attach to perceived threats in order to neutralize them. In MS, antibodies mistakenly attack the myelin on nerve cells. |
| **autoimmune disease** | A disorder that results in loss of function or destruction of normal tissue due to attack by the body's immune system. |
| **axons** | Elongated fibers of neurons that enhance the speed of transmission of nerve impulses from one neuron to another. They are wrapped in myelin, which gets damaged by MS. |
| **central nervous system (CNS)** | Nerve complex consisting of the brain and the spinal cord. |
| **demyelination** | Loss of myelin that surrounds axons or other nerve fibers. In multiple sclerosis the demyelination occurs within the central nervous system. |
| **hyperbaric oxygen** | Oxygen provided at a pressure greater than the normal background atmosphere; some claim success in treating MS with this technology. |
| **inflammation** | Redness, swelling, heat, and pain in a tissue due to, among other things, an allergic reaction. |
| **magnetic resonance imaging (MRI)** | A medical imaging technique that reveals the state of internal soft tissues by using magnetism, radio waves, and a computer to produce the images of body structures. It can be useful in diagnosing MS. |

| | |
|---|---|
| **multiple sclerosis (MS)** | An autoimmune disease in which the body's immune system attacks myelin, a fatty substance that insulates nerves to help in the transmission of nerve signals. It results in a wide variety of symptoms, including numbness, weakness, loss of muscle coordination, and problems with vision, speech, and bladder control. |
| **myelin** | A fatty material composed of regularly alternating membranes that composes the sheath surrounding nerve endings. |
| **neurologist** | A physician who is a specialist in the diagnosis and treatment of disorders of the neuromuscular system, including the central nervous system. |
| **progressive** | In the context of MS, the term means increasing in scope or severity; that is, a disease that is progressing from bad to worse. |
| **sclerosis** | A hardening of tissues in a certain region. |
| **spasticity** | A change in muscles characterized by increasing tightness and rigidity, as well as exaggerated reflexes. |

# CHRONOLOGY

**B.C.**   ca. 370   Hippocrates, the founder of Greek medicine, discusses a disease that causes palsy (or shaking), which might possibly be multiple sclerosis (MS).

**A.D.**   ca. 170   Greek physician Galen provides the first anatomical studies of the brain, based on examination of wounded gladiators and on dissection of animals.

   1824   French physiologist René Dutrochet discovers that all living tissue is composed of cells.

   1860   French researcher Louis-Antoine Ranvier discovers myelin, the insulating sheath that covers nerve cells.

       French neurologist Jean-Martin Charcot first describes multiple sclerosis as a distinct disease characterized by spasticity.

   1864   German researcher Carl Frommann publishes the first medical illustrations of MS lesions.

   1889   The discovery of antibodies provides the first indication of how the body's immune system works—and how it can go wrong.

   1928   Nobel laureate Santiago Ramón y Cajal discovers the role of special cells called oligodendrocytes in coating nerve cells with myelin.

**1937**   Researchers show that when myelin is lost nerve cells have trouble receiving and transmitting impulses.

**1965**   Immune cells called T-cells are found to react against myelin in a process mimicking MS.

**1973**   CAT scan provides the first image of an MS lesion in a living patient.

**1975**   For the first time, researchers identify a specific genetic predisposition to multiple sclerosis.

**1981**   MRI scans provide detailed images of MS in the brain of a living patient.

**1993**   A drug called betaseron wins early approval for treatment of MS.

**1996**   A recombinant interferon drug called Avonex is approved for the treatment of multiple sclerosis. Other drugs soon follow.

**2007**   Two studies discover another gene linked to MS. It is the first such advance in understanding the cause of the disease in thirty years.

# ORGANIZATIONS TO CONTACT

The editors have compiled the following list of organizations concerned with the issues debated in this book. The descriptions are derived from materials provided by the organizations. All have publications or information available for interested readers. The list was compiled on the date of publication of the present volume; the information provided here may change. Be aware that many organizations take several weeks or longer to respond to inquiries, so allow as much time as possible.

**Consortium of Multiple Sclerosis Centers**
359 Main St., Ste. A
Hackensack, NJ 07601
(201) 487-1050
fax: (201) 678-2290
www.mscare.org

The Consortium of Multiple Sclerosis Centers is the leading professional organization for multiple sclerosis health care providers and researchers in North America. It also does global outreach to the MS community with the aim of maximizing the ability of MS health care providers to impact care of people who are affected by MS.

**International Organization of Multiple Sclerosis Nurses**
PO Box 450
Teaneck, NJ 07666
(201) 487-1050
fax: (201) 678-2291
e-mail: info@iomsn.org
www.iomsn.org

The International Organization of Multiple Sclerosis Nurses aims to establish and perpetuate a specialized branch of nursing dedicated to treatment of multiple sclerosis. It works to establish standards of nursing care in multiple sclerosis, to support multiple sclerosis nursing research, and to educate the health care community about multiple sclerosis.

**Multiple Sclerosis
Association of
America (MSAA)**
706 Haddonfield Rd.
Cherry Hill, NJ 08002
(800) 532-7667
fax: (856) 661-9797
e-mail: webmaster@
msassociation.org
www.msassociation.org

The MSAA works to enrich the quality of life for people affected by multiple sclerosis. Its programs and services bring ongoing support and direct services to people with MS and their families throughout the United States. MSAA also serves to promote greater understanding of multiple sclerosis and the diverse needs and challenges of people with MS.

**The Multiple
Sclerosis Foundation**
6350 N. Andrews Ave.
Fort Lauderdale, FL
33309-2130
(800) 225-6495
fax: (954) 938-8708
e-mail: admin@
msfocus.org
www.msfocus.org

The Multiple Sclerosis Foundation provides a comprehensive approach to helping people with MS maintain both their health and well-being. It offers programming and support to people affected by MS, regional support groups, and health care professionals. It maintains a toll-free helpline staffed by caseworkers and peer counselors, as well as online information in both English and Spanish.

**Multiple Sclerosis
International
Federation (MSIF)**
3rd Fl. Skyline House
200 Union St.
London SE1 0LX
United Kingdom
44 (0) 20 7620 1911
fax: 44 (0) 20 7620 1922
e-mail: info@msif.org
www.msif.org

MSIF was established in 1967 to be a global leader in stimulating scientific research into the understanding and treatment of MS and improving quality of life for people affected by MS.

**Multiple Sclerosis
Society of Canada**
175 Bloor St. E.
Ste. 700, North Tower
Toronto, Ontario
M4W 3R8
(416) 922-6065
fax: (416) 922-7538
e-mail: info@
mssociety.ca
www.mssociety.ca

The Multiple Sclerosis Society of Canada is a membership-based organization that seeks to be a leader in finding a cure for multiple sclerosis and enabling people affected by MS to enhance their quality of life. It supports MS research and services that assist people with MS and their families. The organization was founded in 1948.

**Myelin Repair
Foundation (MRF)**
18809 Cox Ave., Ste. 190
Saratoga, CA 95070
(408) 871-2410
fax: (408) 871-2409
e-mail: info@
myelinrepair.org
www.myelinrepair.org

MRF is a nonprofit research foundation dedicated to accelerating basic medical research into myelin repair treatments that will dramatically improve the lives of people suffering from multiple sclerosis. To achieve this goal, MRF has developed a unique business/science hybrid model for medical research to speed the time of drug discovery.

**National Institute of
Neurological
Disorders and Stroke
(NINDS)**
PO Box 5801
Bethesda, MD 20824
(800) 352-9424
e-mail: WebManagers@
ninds.nih.gov
www.ninds.nih.gov

NINDS is one of the more than two dozen research institutes and centers that the National Institutes of Health (NIH) comprises. NINDS conducts and supports research on brain and nervous system disorders, including multiple sclerosis. It provides grants to public and private institutions and individuals for relevant research and programs.

**The National Multiple Sclerosis Society**
733 Third Ave.
New York, NY 10017
(212) 986-3240
www.nationalms society.org

The National Multiple Sclerosis Society is a membership-based organization with chapters in all fifty states in the United States. The society helps people affected by MS by funding research, driving change through advocacy, facilitating professional education, and providing programs and services that help people with MS and their families move their lives forward.

# FOR FURTHER READING

**Books**

Margaret Blackstone, *The First Year: Multiple Sclerosis; An Essential Guide for the Newly Diagnosed.* New York: Marlowe, 2007.

Patricia K. Coyle, *Living with Progressive Multiple Sclerosis: Overcoming the Challenges.* New York: Demos Medical, 2008.

Loren Fishman, *Yoga and Multiple Sclerosis: A Journey to Health and Healing.* New York: Demos Medical, 2007.

Kym Orsetti Furney, *When the Diagnosis Is Multiple Sclerosis: Help, Hope, and Insights from an Affected Physician.* Westport, CT: Praeger, 2008.

Brad Hamler, *Exercises for Multiple Sclerosis: A Safe and Effective Program to Fight Fatigue, Build Strength, and Improve Balance.* New York: Healthylivingbooks, 2006.

Nancy J. Holland, *Multiple Sclerosis: A Guide for the Newly Diagnosed.* New York: Demos Medical, 2007.

Nicholas LaRocca, *Multiple Sclerosis: Understanding the Cognitive Challenges.* New York: Demos Medical, 2006.

Lorna Moorhead, *Phone in the Fridge: Five Years with Multiple Sclerosis.* Tucson, AZ: Pathfinder, 2006.

Louis J. Rosner, *Multiple Sclerosis: New Hope and Practical Advice for People with MS and Their Families.* New York: Simon & Schuster, 2008.

Randall T. Schapiro, *Managing the Symptoms of Multiple Sclerosis.* Berkeley: CA Publishers Group West, 2007.

Allison Shadday, *MS and Your Feelings: Handling the Ups and Downs of Multiple Sclerosis.* Alameda, CA: Hunter House, 2007.

Colin Lee Talley, *A History of Multiple Sclerosis.* Westport, CT: Praeger, 2008.

## Periodicals

Anat Achiron, "Immune Therapy Appears to Reduce Risk of Second Attack of Multiple Sclerosis Symptoms," *Medical News Today*, October 12, 2006. www.medicalnewstoday.com/articles/14807.php.

American Academy of Neurology, "Multiple Sclerosis Is Increasingly Becoming a Woman's Disease: Why?" *ScienceDaily*, April 29, 2007. www.sciencedaily.com/releases/2007/04/070427072325.htm.

American Roentgen Ray Society, "Ultra-High-Field MRI Allows for Earlier Diagnosis of Multiple Sclerosis," *ScienceDaily*, May 6, 2007. www.sciencedaily.com/releases/2007/05/070504121140.htm.

Kavitha Arms, "My Silver Lining," *Newsweek*, September 28, 2007. www.newsweek.com/id/43236.

Jane Brody, "From Multiple Sclerosis, a Multiplicity of Challenges," *New York Times*, March 4, 2008. www.nytimes.com/2008/03/04/health/04brod.html.

The Canadian Press, "Presence of Other Health Conditions Delays Diagnosis of MS, Study Suggests," October 29, 2008. www.canadianpress.com.

Peter M. Crosta, "Multiple Sclerosis Activity May Be Affected by Prozac," *Medical News Today*, May 3, 2008. www.medicalnewstoday.com/articles/106150.php.

Kathleen Doheny, "Caffeine Could Stave Off Multiple Sclerosis," *U.S. News & World Report*, June 30, 2008.

Ed Edelson, "Red Wine Molecule Might Battle MS," *Washington Post*, September 19, 2008. www.washingtonpost.com/wp-dyn/content/article/2008/09/19/AR2008091901081.html.

Gwen Ericson, "Interferon Could Be a Key to Preventing or Treating Multiple Sclerosis," *Washington University School of Medicine News*, October 29, 2008. http://mednews.wustl.edu/news/page/normal/12859.html.

E.M. Frohman, M.K. Racke, and C.S. Raine, "Medical Progress: Multiple Sclerosis—the Plaque and Its Pathogenesis," *New England Journal of Medicine*, March 2, 2006.

Amanda Gardner, "Multiple Sclerosis Drug May Be Linked to Melanoma," *Washington Post*, February 6, 2008. www .washingtonpost.com/wp-dyn/content/article/2008/02/06/ AR2008020603459.html.

Jeneen Interlandi, "One Piece of a Terrible Puzzle," *Newsweek*, July 29, 2007.

International Multiple Sclerosis Genetics Consortium, "Risk Alleles for Multiple Sclerosis Identified by a Genomewide Study," *New England Journal of Medicine*, August 30, 2007.

Marjorie Lazoff, "Multiple Sclerosis," *eMedicine.com*, March 3, 2008. www.emedicine.com/emerg/TOPIC321.HTM.

Amy Maxmen, "Pathology of Multiple Sclerosis Determined by Response to Immune Protein," *Medical News Today*, October 14, 2008. www.medicalnewstoday.com/articles/125342.php.

Trine Rasmussen Nielsen et al., "Multiple Sclerosis After Infectious Mononucleosis," *Archives of Neurology*, January 1, 2007.

Alice Park, "New Genes Discovered for MS," *Time*, July 29, 2007. www.time.com/time/health/article/0,8599,1647940, 00.html.

Andrew Pollack, "F.D.A. Approves a Multiple Sclerosis Drug," *New York Times*, November 24, 2004. www.nytimes.com/ 2004/11/24/business/24pharma.html.

Gregory J. Roehrich, "On Pins and Needles," *Newsweek*, February 26, 2008. www.newsweek.com/id/115405.

# INDEX

A

Allergen-free diets, 62–63, 102

Aloe vera, 104

Alternative therapies, 32, *97*

American Academy of Neurology, 71–72

Amitriptyline, 46

Anthocyanosides, 64, 65

Anti-candida (yeast infection) treatment, 100

Antidepressants, 47, 59, 104

Antioxidants, 65

Autoimmune diseases, 18
  food allergens and, 63–64
  genetic factors in, 26–27

B

Bee stings, 33–34, 105

Betaseron, 87

Binding antibodies (BAbs), 46

Bipolar disorder, 57–58

Blood-brain barrier (BBB), 62, *68*, 76
  activated T cells crossing, 69
  chemicals strengthening, 64
  head trauma and breakdown in, 69–70
  MRI showing breakdown in, *68*

Boggild, Mike, 49

Booker, Wendy, 124

Brodsky, Ruthan, 16

C

Calcium, 104

Cambridge diet, 103

Campath (alemtuzumab), 49

Carter, Joan, 9

Cellular therapy, 105

Centers for Disease Control and Prevention (CDC), 28

Cerebrosides, 104

Charcot, Jean-Martin, 74, *74*

*Chlamydia Pneumoniae,* 30

Cognition, MS and changes in, 21

Cohen, Richard M., 116, *120*

Colostrum, hyperimmune, 104

Computerized tomography (CT), 41

Corticosteroids. *See* Steroids

D

Dardik, Irving I., 12–14

Dental fillings, 99–100

Depression, 21, 104
  varieties of, 56–58

Diet/dietary therapy
  allergen-free, 63–64, 102
  appears to help MS patients, 96–100
  featuring immune-enhancing foods, 64–66
  fructose-restricted, 103
  low-fat, 64

Tysabri (natalizumab), 47–48, *48*

U
Undersea and Hyperbaric Medical
   Society, 91

V
Viruses, 27-28
   autoimmunity induced by, 19
   suspected, in MS, 28–30, 75–76
Visual evoked potential (VEP), 42

Vitamin B$_{12}$, 98
Vitamin C, 104
Vitamin D, 104
Vitamins, 103

W
Weatherby, S.J.M., 67
Whiplash injury, 70

Y
Yoga, *32*